valerie Be

Getting Out of Your
kids' Faces and

Into Their
Hearts

Become the Warm,
Loving Parent You've Always
Wanted to Be

MOTHERS OF
M♥PS.
PRESCHOOLERS

ZondervanPublishingHouse
Grand Rapids, Michigan

A Division of HarperCollinsPublishers

Getting Out of Your Kids' Faces & Into Their Hearts
Copyright © 1994 by Valerie Bell

Requests for information should be addressed to:
Zondervan Publishing House
Grand Rapids, Michigan 49530

Library of Congress Cataloging-in-Publication Data

Bell, Valerie, 1949–
    Getting out of your kids' faces and into their hearts / Valerie Bell.
      p.   cm.
    ISBN 0-310-48451-0 (pbk.)
    1. Parent and child. 2. Parenting.   I. Title.
    HQ755.85.B45 1995
    649'.1—dc20   94-30678
                                                     CIP

Interior design by Sue Koppenol

Printed in the United States of America

  98 99 00 01 02 / ❖ DC / 10 9 8 7 6 5 4

To you, my family.

To Steve, my parenting partner.
Thank you for ordering our lives. Your love and nurture
strengthen us every day.

To Brendan and Justin! My sons.
Thank you for home schooling me in a hands-on course
in parenting during these family years.

You three are the best "Boys' Club" a woman
ever was allowed to join!

To you!
My thanks! My love! You're the best!.

Getting Out of Your
Kids' Faces and

Into Their
Hearts

Other books by Valerie Bell

Coming Back: Real-Life Stories of Courage from Spiritual Survivors,
    with Steve Bell
Reaching Out to Lonely Kids: A Guide to Surviving and Loving
    the Children in Your Neighborhood
She Can Laugh at the Days to Come

CONTENTS

INTRODUCTION
Where Successful Parenting Begins

Being a parent is like trying to put an enormous family jigsaw puzzle together. There are so many pieces, where do you begin? Where does the discipline piece fit? What can you overlook, if anything, and what should you never fail to address? Pieces called bedtime and manners and appropriate behavior beg to be put into their proper spots. Yet how can a parent fit the puzzle pieces of "Eat your carrots and peas" with the "I love you" pieces and have it all make sense?

Well into their family years, many parents suspect that their family puzzle seems to be missing pieces, or that the pieces seem to be mismatched. Despite incredible effort, the puzzle stubbornly refuses to come together.

With diligent work and the best of intentions, many parents succeed only in frustrating themselves and their children. No one works harder with less success than a parent who is clueless about the design of this puzzle called family. More and more they are "in their kids' faces" instead of "into their hearts." Their family life is unbelievably stressful. Still, parents know the pieces can't just be put back in a box and forgotten about. The puzzle must be solved, and it can be if parents are open to changing what hasn't been working. We can take a clue from jigsaw puzzle experts: Start with the border. The border helps the other pieces fall right into place. Instead of an enormous frustration, with a completed border the puzzle now becomes a joy to fit together.

What is the border, what are the pieces parents must learn to put in place before all other aspects of family life? Trust. Nurture. Relationship.

"I'm crazy about you!" is the message of these border pieces. Amid schedules and training, feeding and clothing, discipline and child management, and the other aspects of family life, how often these most important pieces fail to be obviously placed, even when it is what the parent is actually feeling. How sad—parents who love and children who fail to receive that most important piece of family life.

Watch the pieces fit in your family when the border of "I'm crazy about you!" is given priority placement. Here are five benefits your family will enjoy as you learn to solve the puzzle through nurturing your relationships—a dynamic often called attachment.

First, *your child will enjoy the greatest of all life advantages.* Without wealth or genius IQ or inherited good looks or remarkable talent, your child will still thrive. Mountains will be seen as challenges, not obstacles; relationships will be entered into with confidence that he or she is lovable and therefore worthy to give and receive love. When your child knows you are crazy about him or her, a sense of well-being will characterize your child even more than his or her more genetically blessed peers. And while any parent can give their children this advantage, your child can be the rare child who actually receives such a daily blessing.

In addition, *discipline becomes a smaller piece of the family puzzle.* "I'm crazy about you!" is the best disciplinary tool a parent has in their whole bag of tricks. It is better than spankings, better than time-outs, better than taking away privileges. Attachment is the positive aspect of child training. An emotionally connected child needs fewer directions, fewer rules, less instruction talk, and fewer spankings. That's because a child who is attached to his or her parents obeys out of honor to that relationship. That is a very different kind of obedience than the obedience that comes because mom or dad is bigger, threatening, or in the room at the time! Attachment leads to obedience that comes from a child's heart. That's the kind of obedience I really want from my children.

Let me describe what this obedience looks like. An incident with my oldest son made me realize something unusually wonderful was happening between us, even though, at the time, I did not know what it was called. He was seven, and had spent the morning playing with several other children his age. After a time, I noticed it had become quiet outside. I looked out the window and was surprised to see him all alone.

"Brendan, where are your friends? Why are you playing by yourself?"

"Oh, Mom, they all decided to go the park across the tracks, and I knew you wouldn't want me to go there, so I stayed here when they left."

I was touched and amazed. He had not even bothered to try to ask me about crossing the railroad tracks. No nagging, no whining, no tears, no accusations. Sue, he had wanted to go, but he knew my values and had obeyed without even having to ask. His heart had honored me that day. Today, I know what to call that. It is attachment. We were an attached parent-child couple. Trust had been established in our relationship.

There's more! *Attachment is the greatest protection you can give your child from negative peer pressure.* In the same way our relationship gave my seven-year-old the strength to say no to friends and practice his mother's values, it gives older children courage to turn from drugs, promiscuity, and other harmful charms. *Attachment also allows a child to trust that mom and dad are looking out for his or her very best.* Believe me, it works better than strict curfews, excessive rules, and unrelenting emotional scenes. In seeking to protect, strictness too often provides the fodder for rebellious fires and achieves the opposite effect. The only sure way to protect your child against perverse influences is through a strong, positive, involved parent-child attached relationship.

Getting this great benefit for your family is what this book is about. The approach is amazingly simple. Learn to ask, "What does this child need?" and then set your heart to need-meeting. Do it ungrudgingly, do it with joy, do it consistently. Get out of your kids' faces with your "more important" agendas, and get into their hearts instead.

Sound like a great plan to become slave to your child's every whim? Well, here is the best news about meeting your children's needs: Attachment will lighten your parental load. Studies show that within the first three years children have already figured out whether or not mom and dad are "crazy" about them. This early message is crucial. Meet your child's early needs, establish a sympathetic relationship, prioritize the message "I am crazy about you" before any other agenda, and you will get what you really want. In the family years to come you will enjoy the closeness you long to feel with your children.

Finally, *attachment is the best gift parents can give this sad world.* Your parenting is the solution to a much larger puzzle. Saint Augustine recognized the impact of parents not only on their own children but on the society at large when he said, "Give me better mothers, and I will give you another world."

Exactly. Give your kids your best motherly self, your most excellent fatherly self. Become skilled at family living. Dream with me that we will someday witness what your family and mine—and this world—so desperately needs: Better mothers and fathers who will have the skills to nurture a trend toward a much better world.

It's never too late. Whether your child is three or thirty, start today getting out of your kids' faces and into their hearts, and then watch as the pieces of your faily life come together in an amazing way. Get ready to receive the blessing of the parent who is raising the rare well-loved child.

By divine design a child has been born to you.
A fragile infant. A girl-child, a boy-child.
Tucked closely, watched carefully, the baby emerges.
Eyes and face and body respond
To you.
You are parent. To your child you are precious.
Soon words are flowing.
You tutor the "pleases" and "thank yous" of manners and etiquette.
But will you teach the language of the heart?
"I love you. You're special and precious
To me."

Tucked closely, watched carefully, the toddler emerges.
Peanut-butter fingers caress your face, baby lips sprinkle your cheeks with
graham-cracker kisses.
For you.
You are parent. To your child you are precious.
Diapers to lunch boxes,
Homework to car keys.
You launder and clean and sign forms and chauffeur,
But will you remember the language of the heart?
"I love you. You're special and precious
To me."

Raised nearly, watched carefully, the adult child emerges.
Have the years drawn you closer, or are you intimate strangers?
You will always be parent, but will you still be precious?
Especially these days, remember the language of the heart.
"I love you. You're special and precious
To me."

VALERIE BELL

PART ONE:

Getting Out of Your Kids' Faces . . .

*Well-loved children are much rarer than one would guess.
Most people in our society unfortunately do not really know
how to love other people well. Children who are well-loved
will mostly grow up to be loving adults.*[1]

GILBERT W. KLIMAN
AND ALBERT ROSENFELD
Responsible Parenthood

ONE

WHEN SOMETHING IS MISSING:
A Crisis In Parental Confidence

I didn't notice her at first. It was that delightful, animated after-class time when people hang around to talk. Asking questions, sharing illustrations, and sometimes challenging what they've heard, eager seminar attendees grab the last few moments to relate to me what's on their minds about the things they've been hearing.

But, for some reason, this young mother hadn't made herself a part of the after-class crowd. During the laughing and storytelling, she had stayed quietly alone in the back of the meeting room. Then as the group dispersed, she walked to the front. I was struck with her apparent sadness. Reaching for my hand and averting her eyes, she sighed, "Mrs. Bell." *When did I become Mrs. Bell?* I wondered. (Weren't we nearly the same age, this young mom and I? I mean, I am only two teenage sons away from sandboxes and big wheels and matchbox cars. That's not enough time to become distanced by formality!)

"Oh, please," I smiled and pleaded, "just call me Valerie!"

She didn't laugh or even smile. Instead, she pressed a folded note into my palm, curled my fingers over the top, and pressed them down.

"Please read this . . . but not until the conference is over."

With that she turned and left the room.

I looked down at the creased paper in my hand. It was moist from sweat. *O God*, I wondered, *what horror story am I going to find at the end of the day when I read this letter? Is she abusing her children? Is her marriage falling apart? What terrible thing has she confided in me?*

I tucked her crumpled page into a safe place in my briefcase, and later that night I retrieved it and read what was breaking her heart.

> Dear Mrs. Bell,
>
> I just had to write you this note. I am the mother of four children, all under eight years old. My husband is the leader of the weekly children's program at our church. We work with the youth group. I even home-school our children. Everyone thinks we are such good parents. But I know we're not. I've read everything I can find about raising children, but still—something is missing. I've never been able to put it into words before today, but what's missing in our home is relationship. We function, but it breaks my heart to realize how much my children have missed because I don't know how to be the warm, loving mother I know they need. Can you please help me?

And she signed her name.

Something's missing . . . because I don't know how to be the warm, loving mother I know my children need.

So that was it! Why had I submitted to her "read it later, please" agenda? Why hadn't I opened the conversational door just a crack? Now, how was I going to help her?

I thought of all the parents I'd met since I first started speaking up about children's problems. In the past few years I have been crisscrossing the country, challenging people to be surrogate parents for the hurting children in their lives, neighborhoods, and church programs— and people are so responsive! Yet, very often, too often, there have been other responses, curious echoes of the sad note that was pressed into my palm that day. These are not admissions of gross abuse but of a struggle within that is serious and fundamental.

- "I can see the importance of Christian adults being committed to 'be there' for children who don't have anyone, but, to tell you the truth, I'm not even sure that I'm a good parent to my own kids!"
- "I'm never sure if I'm doing things right. There are times when I feel so defeated. Is parenting supposed to be this hard?"
- "My kids drive me crazy. What started as a love relationship has turned into mutual resentment. At night I know they sometimes lie in bed angry at me, and I guess, although I'm ashamed to admit it, I feel the same about them."

The comments above remind me of one writer's description of the relationship between a mother and her demanding offspring.

- "The baby is an interference with her private life. . . . He is ruthless, treats her as scum, an unpaid servant, a slave.

  His excited love is cupboard love, so that having got what he wants he throws her away like an orange peel.

  He is suspicious, refuses her good food, and makes her doubt herself, but he eats well with his aunt.

  After an awful morning with him, she goes out, and he smiles at a stranger, who says: 'Isn't he sweet?'

If she fails him at the start, she knows he will pay her out forever."[2] Or this mother's honest admission:

- "I am angry at my baby," she says, describing the end of a long, hard mothering day. "I yell into his little face for his endless crying and throw him roughly into his crib. Then I quickly sweep him into my arms, protecting him from his insane mother, fearing that I will . . . drive my child crazy. For if I interpret the experts correctly, this is not a hard thing to do."[3]

I've also heard the following comments, which reflect the self-image problem parents experience after dealing nose to nose with a child day after day.

- "I used to be a nice person. Now A.K. (after kids) I've turned into a raving, screaming, out-of-control witch. I don't even like myself anymore . . . no wonder my kids keep their distance."

- "I'm the strong-willed parent of a strong-willed child. Relationally we are at a stand-off, and worst of all, I suspect I'm the one who taught him everything he knows."

Nagging questions lurk behind all of the previous comments, "Am I a good parent, or not? Should I be feeling these strong negative feelings?" In many different ways I'm hearing parents say that something has gone wrong. Parenting isn't what they thought it was going to be. Their words convey a terrible sense of shame, defeat, and disappointment they feel with themselves as parents.

Are these parents just expressing the "normal" emotional gap that occurs between the exciting commitment we feel when we bring our babies home from the hospital, when everything's new and smelling of baby powder and full of possibilities, and all those necessary, messy-diaper-filled, peanut butter-and-jelly-sticky dull days of duty that follow? Are they simply expressing their disappointment with the disparity that exists between their ideal and the actual reality of family life?

Maybe.

Another possibility. Perhaps they really are good parents, but they don't know it.

How do any of us know if we're good parents? There are no job evaluations, no family-living report cards. The only input most of us receive is from our kids, and they have been known to be somewhat biased in their reporting!

One of my sons had a charming way of inserting and twisting the knife of child feedback about my parenting. With the sweetest voice and the most endearing smile he would deliver this line—"You're the best mommy in the whole world—except for this one little thing . . ." Then he would proceed to let me know what he *really* thought of my mothering!

Or perhaps there is a third possibility. These parents may have developed certain adult skills—they are adept at being "good people," they make adult friends, function in an adult job market, pay their bills, and meet their obligations—but somehow they've missed out on another whole set of skills: the ones needed to be "good parents."

However you account for it, there is no doubt in my mind that many of us are experiencing a real crisis in confidence about our ability to parent. Until now, when I've met parents who are in a full-blown crisis of confidence, I've also been frustrated—frustrated that with limited time, all I've been able to give them is an encouraging word and a reminder that we all find raising a family to be a challenging job.

That's pretty shallow comfort for someone who feels that he or she is failing at the most important job one will ever have!

When you're a parent who senses that "something is missing," you may feel frustrated—as if everyone knows a basic fact about parenting of which you are somehow totally unaware. It's like having an important secret withheld.

When you're a parent who's "read all the books" but still can't seem to "connect" with the children who mean more to you than anything else in the world, you may feel that something is intrinsically wrong with you. You might feel a deep sense of inner shame.

When other parents seem to "have it together" while you struggle with getting through the day in one piece, you might feel a sense of defeat, that you are just unequipped for your parental role. You might conclude that you are inadequate, compared with other more skilled parents you know.

Maybe you are experiencing a crisis in confidence that is so deeply painful you can hardly bring yourself to talk about it to anyone. Maybe you don't ask for input because it would mean exposing yourself and being vulnerable. Besides, you despair that anyone can really help.

Let me reassure you. I believe it's possible to *learn* how to be a good parent—because parenting is a skill that *can* be acquired. Yes, some people are more naturally gifted in parenting, that's true. Just as there are world-class athletes, writers, musicians, there are world-class parents— people who are better at the art of parenting intrinsically. But they simply know by instinct—perhaps by modeling from their own childhoods—"secrets" about the parental role. If you feel inadequate as a parent, then you need to know that you can learn those secrets no matter what your background.

You can find out what's missing. You can self-educate. In fact, I believe that some of the best parents are those who have learned parenting, not just come by it naturally. We all know many parents who are doing a great job but who were themselves raised in homes where "something was missing." It's as if they remember what was painfully lacking in their own childhoods and are making the effort to be sure that it is not missing in their adult homes with their own children.

I visited such a home recently. The young father had shared his history of abuse at the hands of his angry mother—his childhood was a nightmare of physical, sexual, and emotional abuse. That day, as I visited with him and his wife in their home, I watched him with his children. He gave bottles and cuddled, changed diapers, and tucked into bed. He seemed delighted with his brood, engaging in a family tradition of turning children into hot dogs between two pillows for buns, tickling them when imaginary mustard and relish and ketchup were added. It was wild and relational and loud! Occasionally he would catch my eye and smile, a smile that said, "Well, it's great to be a parent, don't you think?"

For the time being, nothing is missing in that home. This young father has found his way despite his own damaged childhood. He had found the way to his own heart. It is my prayer that he will hold true during all the "uncharted" years of family life ahead of him. It is also my hope that this book will help you who may sense the need to have "something more" in your family, find the way to your own heart.

A HOPEFUL PROMISE

I love the verse that ends the Old Testament. It speaks to a deep human yearning. With this sweet promise, God closed the Old Testament and began the silent intertestamental period. With these last important words—the words he wanted remembered—he touched a deep chord: "He shall turn the hearts of the fathers to their children, and the hearts of the children to their fathers . . ."

> May your dreams of a close family life be realized, and may that dream begin with you.

My prayer is that your spirit will join mine in saying, "We're ready! Ready for that heart job, God! Fulfill that sweet promise in our families. And above all else, start with me. I'm ready for something more!"

For the sad-eyed young mother who pressed her desire to be "the warm, loving mother my children need" into my hand that day, for the young father enjoying playing "human hot dog" with his children as he turns from his abused past, and for all the others I've met who've expressed a desire for getting closer to their children, I want to share the things I know about becoming a relational parent. I hope these ideas will help you in the uncharted years of family life ahead of you. I hope it will inspire you to become the parent you want to be, the parent your children *need* you to be.

I write with compassion for you if in your past "something may have been missing," with empathy for your struggle to be a more-skilled parent, and with a great desire for you to experience closeness with your children during these intense family years. Here's to you! Here's to the ones you love! May your dreams of a close family life be realized, and may that dream begin with you.

On one occasion, when I was furious with my son, I took a favorite trophy of his and threw it on the floor. Of course, it was irreplaceable and broke to bits. It never occurred to me that I was experiencing the same feelings of rage, frustration, and inability to cope, hopelessness, and helplessness that causes many parents to harm their children, sometimes severely. I do know that, like most mothers, I could have used a lot of help when my children were little because, despite my B.A. and my M.A. and even my teaching experience, I knew nothing about caring for a child.[1]

NAOMI FEIGELSON CHASE
A Child Is Being Beaten

TWO

HOW DO I KNOW IF I'M A GOOD PARENT?

Understanding the Bottom Line

Here's a classic scene, one sure to erode parental confidence: My fifteen-year-old son, Justin, and I were shopping in a mall. Suddenly we heard, then saw a two-year-old screaming and rolling on the ground right in front of Mrs. Field's Cookies. The little "darling" wanted a chocolate-chip cookie *without* nuts! He was angry! He was loud! He was a two-year-old version of Conan the Barbarian!

I glanced at his mom. She was embarrassed; she looked haggard. I knew what she was thinking. *"If I were a GOOD mom, my child wouldn't be having this temper tantrum here in front of Mrs. Field's Cookies!"*

I looked directly at my son and said, "That poor mother!"

In less time than it takes to inhale he shot back, "Yeah, that poor kid!"

Touché! He had me! The quality of parenting is very definitely a matter of perspective.

KIDS HAVEN'T CHANGED THAT MUCH—HAVE WE?

Adults have always struggled in dealing with children. Socrates described children of his time: "Children today are tyrants. They contradict their parents, gobble their food, and tyrannize their teachers." That quote not only amuses me, but it reminds me that children haven't changed much down through the years. He could be describing my children or yours! I'm somehow perversely comforted by that.

It also makes me wish that history had left us a similar quote from some wise child about parents. Would it be interchangeable with some of the things children say today about parents? Or have we parents evolved and progressed in our roles? With all our education, with everything that's studied and written and communicated about parenting, with all the material available to us on the topic of raising children, have we developed to a more-skilled level of parenting than, say, Socrates' peers, or even the generation of parents just ahead of us?

Or have we parents not changed all that much, either?

As educated, knowledgeable citizens of the most civilized culture ever, how much do we know about good parenting?

TEST FOR CITIZENS OF A CIVILIZED CULTURE

Let me try an experiment with you to demonstrate what I mean. Can you answer the following questions?

First, can you recite the Pledge of Allegiance? Yes, you probably can. Why? Because, when we were growing up, our government decided that it was important for children living in the United States to understand a basic credo about what it means to be an American. So all across America, children in classrooms put their hands over their hearts and pledge their loyalty to the American flag.

Second question: Can you hum, sing, or recite a McDonald's or Burger King commercial?

Of course you can. Our free-enterprise system and its billion-dollar advertising industry has made sure those ideas are nailed down in our heads. You probably didn't even have to think very hard about it—you could easily pull those phrases out of your consciousness.

You see, we tend as a society to define and get across the values we cherish.

So far, you're probably two for two. You can recite the Pledge of Allegiance—that means you know the basics of good citizenry; you're familiar with some hamburger commercials—that means you're versed in American marketing through jingoism.

> Think about it. We have driving schools, cooking schools, schools for auctioneers, schools for scuba divers, schools of higher education, beauty schools, support groups for every conceivable human problem—we even take our dogs to obedience school—but where do we go to learn how to be good parents? Why don't we have parenting schools?

Here's something that shouldn't be that difficult to answer. It's basic. It's fundamental.

Can you give a one-sentence definition of good parenting?

Can't come up with one right off the top of your head? All right, put this book down and take as long as you want to do some research. Try to find a basic working definition of good parenting. Eventually you might find one. My point is, the working definition for this basic human relationship—a role that so affects the health of our society and our world—is hardly on the tip of anyone's tongue!

No wonder we're in the midst of a parental "confidence crisis!" *If we aren't sure what good parenting is, how do we know if we are adequate and measuring up?*

IS RAISING WELL-LOVED CHILDREN IMPORTANT TO US?

Think about it. We have driving schools, cooking schools, schools for auctioneers, schools for scuba divers, schools of higher education, beauty schools, support groups for every conceivable human problem—we even take our dogs to obedience school—but where do we go to learn how to be good parents? Why don't we have parenting schools?

Perhaps we have held on to a deep-seated belief that parenting can't be taught. Our usual approach to family problems is remedial, "after-the-damage" help. But for many families such help is too little too late. The troubled-family snowball is gaining enormous momentum in our time. Too often, remedial help is like putting a Band-Aid on a hemorrhage. It would be infinitely better for both the family and the culture to put more effort into prescriptive help.

WEIGHED DOWN BY MISINFORMATION

Unfortunately, the lack of education about parenting creates a vacuum into which misinformation flows. Confusion abounds. Instead of receiving accurate information about good parenting, we are often left with societal "myths" and misinformation that create numerous problems for Moms and Dads. In *How to Be a Good Mom*, Stephen and Janet Bly compiled a list of some of the myths we hold on to about good mothering:

A good mom:

- Appears instantly whenever any family member yells, "Mom!"
- Knows exactly which garment each child wants to wear to school each day and has it washed, mended, and hung in the closet
- Never raises her voice
- Attends every T-ball and soccer game in hose and heels (fresh from the office or some other world-expanding venture)
- Never leaves kids with runny noses in the church nursery.
- Never says no to the PTA
- Keeps a regimented family schedule of daily tooth-flossing and Bible memorization[2]

Should we be surprised with these kinds of expectations that we often feel burdened and incompetent in our role as parents?

Add to that unfocused approach the wear and tear of dealing with children every day (kids make our job so tough!) and there you have it—a major case for parental insecurity.

CHILD MANAGEMENT—THE TRADITIONAL APPROACH

Well, what's a poor mom or poor dad to do? Suppose you were the mom standing in front of Mrs. Field's cookies while your toddler was throwing a fit? What would you do?

The "experts" have differing approaches. Much has been written about managing the temper tantrums of two-year-olds. Take your pick.

Some caution that toddlers who are dragged around malls, missing their naps, tend to become crabby. So, avoid the tired-toddler mall scenario entirely.

Other authorities warn us not to discipline in public but to be sure that our little ones understand that there will be private consequences for public outbursts.

Still others counsel parents to divert a toddler's attention by teaching delayed gratification. ("You go to three stores with me, and then we'll go to the pet store—or the store of your choice.") You know, good old bribery!

All of these experts are talking about child management—techniques to get a kid to be civilized enough so we can stand being with him or her.

Now, I am not minimizing this kind of help. We need such guidance for sure, but if you're like me, you don't want simply to manage your children. I certainly don't want my kids to think of me as just the Queen of Child Management. "There's good old Mom. March! 2–3–4. About-face! 2–3–4. At the whistle—on the snap! Brush! Floss! Comb! Pick up!"

Yeah, good old Mom! And Dad, wasn't he the best sergeant a kid ever had?

No, I don't want simply to manage my children. I want my children to love me. I want deep emotional and spiritual closeness. I want parenting to be a relational journey, not just an exercise in "little people" control.

I suspect that's what you really want, too.

I sat down recently and wrote out a list of what I *really* want from my children. Here it is—a little idealistic, I admit, but honest just the same:

- I want them to *like* being with me—even at the mall!
- I want them occasionally to prefer spending time with me to spending time with their friends. (After all—I'm the one who's been crazy about them since they were in utero! Why should I *always* play second fiddle to one of their pubescent peers who wears a baseball cap backward, litters our family room with pop cans and junk-food wrappers, who reeks of Old Spice, whose primary charms seem to be the ability to ollie on a skateboard and the knowledge of the secret codes

in Super Mario Brothers? I mean, if I can't compete with *that*, I might as well hang it up!)

- I want them to hold my hand in public—even when they're thirteen! (Okay—even I can see that that's highly out of the question. Instead, I'd settle for having them walk *beside* me instead of a block behind.)
- I want us to laugh together. A lot.
- I want us to share Cokes without their first wiping my lipstick from the straw with a disgusted expression on their faces.
- I want to dance with them to my oldies music at night. I want to wear Groucho masks to breakfast and act like nothing's unusual.
- I want them to tell me all their deep dark secrets and dreams—and I do mean *all* of them.
- I want them to ask me for advice—and then follow it!
- I want them to quote me and brag about me to their teachers.
- I want them to think that I am not only funny, smart, and beautiful —but extremely spiritual as well!
- I want to feel so close to them that it hurts.

That's all I really want! I don't just want to win the child-management wars. I want intimate emotional and spiritual closeness. That's what I thought I was getting into when I brought those babies home from the hospital!

Isn't that what you long for? More than just knowing how to control a two-year-old, we parents want to connect, to understand, and to be understood. We want a mutual attachment—to love and to be loved in return. We want to lie down at night and not feel brokenhearted with the nagging awareness that our child dislikes us. Or even more important, we want to love our children purely without feelings of resentment—or something that sometimes feels awfully close to hatred on our part.

I believe that's the missing piece that these young parents have been talking about. Though without realizing it, they're asking "How do I *emotionally connect* with my children?"

I believe it's the missing piece that one older mother spoke of when she confided that her biggest mistake in raising her children was that she was consumed with the logistics of everyday living—making sure their clothes were ironed, that they had hot meals, car-pooling them to all their activities. "I spent too much time *on* my kids, not *with* them," she said.[3]

A NEW APPROACH

Much is written about child rearing, child discipline, and child management, but little is available on the emotional, spiritual, and relational issues between parent and child. Perhaps it's time for a different approach.

So, are you a good parent? Do you function simply on a child-management level? Then you might be an adequate parent—one who gets the job done but fails to be aware of or to address the emotional and relational issues between yourself and your children. Or are you the exceptional parent—one who's keenly aware that there's more to raising children than training? How aware are you of the emotional and relational aspects to parenting?

This book is for parents who want to be exceptionally good with their children. The target audience is the parent who wants to raise the rare well-loved child. You will need to know what makes the difference between *adequate* and *exceptional* parenting. What is that seemingly indefinable element that separates good parents from simply adequate parents? What is the parental focal point that helps us to connect with our children—that encourages relational attachment? What would I make sure is taught in "parenting school"? What is the anchor I would give to parents adrift on the sea of parental insecurity?

This: *Good parenting is becoming aware of the physical, emotional, and spiritual needs of a child and meeting those needs.*

A good parent is a nurturer. Or more simply: A good parent is a *need-meeter.*

The apostle Paul teaches parents to raise up their children in the *nurture* and admonition of the Lord (Ephesians 6:4 KJV). Admonition is the side of parenting that emphasizes discipline and training. You could call it the child-management part of parenting.

But Paul couples *admonition* with *nurture.* Raising children was never meant to be divorced from the softening influence of nurture. In my years of working with and observing Christian family systems, this is the most common and ultimately disastrous mistake made in the name of Christian parenting. *We are managing our children right out of our lives.* In our attempts to raise them to be Christian and obedient, as we enroll them in Bible memory programs, while we home school and Sunday school them, while we focus on training them, as we discipline, correct, and mold them to be straight—we may tragically "miss" relationship with our children along the way.

There is another danger. Children raised with the admonition of the Lord, with little nurture of the Lord, are more apt to reject their parents' Christian values.

THE MANAGED BUT POORLY NURTURED CHRISTIAN CHILD

My hometown was a laboratory for studying different Christian family styles. There were many Christian families and many kinds of parents. Some families were heavy on the management side of raising their children. I particularly remember one family in which the parents were extremely controlling. They rarely smiled. They were scandalized by other Christian parents' "leniency." Their daughters were not allowed to participate in worldly activities at the public school. School plays were out. As were cheerleading and drill team. Makeup was forbidden. As was dating. Their daughters were raised straight, not through their own choice but by the management style of their parents. For a while, their children bought in. One daughter wrote in someone else's yearbook, "I hope you get your life straightened out."

But something went wrong. Several years out of high school, that daughter threw all of her parents' values aside and moved in with her boyfriend. She also threw her parents aside. Her parents had managed her right out of their lives. Her needs were not considered. Their rules were what mattered.

This is just one example. And although my generation of Christian children have exited Christianity at alarming rates, we continue in the same family patterns. I see disciplined, managed Christian children everywhere. I grieve that they are missing the soft nurturing side of their parents that would allow them to attach not only to their parents' values but to their parents themselves.

It's tragic, isn't it? Especially when you realize how far such parenting falls from God's ideal system. The family plan, in God's design, was that parents would understand not only the training aspect of parenting but what it means to nurture a child. It is the key to the way he created our human emotional makeup.

HAVING YOUR NEEDS MET: THE FOUNDATION FOR TRUSTING RELATIONSHIPS

From a child's primary relationship with his or her parent flows that child's future ability to love and trust. It's fundamental to a child's quality of life that we learn to be the "warm, loving mothers and fathers they need."

A good parent is a nurturer.

A nurturing parent can be trusted to meet a child's needs. The exceptionally good parent is one who understands what a child needs and delivers it consistently. A pattern of predictable, dependable nurture develops a trust bond between parent and child. It's the closest thing to the Garden of Eden that most of us will ever know on earth. A child who can trust his or her parent to anticipate his or her needs is a secure child. A child whose needs for emotional closeness and comfort are met is a child who can enjoy a sense of well-being. A child who senses that he is his parents' first priority—before any other thing feels secure. A secure child is less apt to act out or develop behavior problems. Between the nurturing parent and the well-cared for child is an exquisite bond that is a beauty to behold—and even more beautiful to experience.

UNDERSTANDING A CHILD'S EMOTIONAL MAKEUP

If your heart leaps a little at that description, if you are motivated to excel in your role as a parent, then you need to understand the emotional makeup of a child in order to understand what a child needs.

A child learns very early whether his or her parents can be trusted and are bond-worthy. The word *bond* refers to the attachment or connection developed between parents and their children. When scientists learned that animal babies bonded (actually, in animals this is called *imprinting*—a kind of animal "love at first sight") at birth with their first caretaker, whether or not it was their natural mother, or even a member of their own species, they began to encourage human mothers to have natural childbirth to begin the bonding process. The immediate care an alert mother could provide her child was thought to greatly strengthen the parent-child bond.

But we are so much more than animals. We don't simply imprint at birth and the bond is forever strong! If that were the case, all babies would be bonded to their mothers, and vice versa, because—face it, we moms still manage to be there at the birthing table! Bonding in the human animal only *begins* at pregnancy and birth. It must be strengthened. It must be nursed. It must be carefully tended.

INVESTING IN THE FAMILY "TRUST BANK"

Maybe you're thinking at this point that we're all doomed to fail as parents. How can we possibly meet our children's every need? It's impossible. Even the best parents will not always meet every need of their children. That's all right. *Attachment is based upon the preponderance of evidence that Mom and Dad are, for the most part, trustworthy.* It's as if we're building a "trust bank." Every time we meet our children's needs, we contribute to the accumulation of trust. I picture the family trust bank as an enormous mound. When my child's need is met, the mound grows. When I fail, I chip away just a little bit at the holdings in the "trust bank."

Did you realize that all that crying of babies and small children is not just about changing diapers, and feeding, and napping? It's a test. Will Mom and Dad figure it out? Are they smart? Can I trust them to understand me? The first three years in a child's life are crucial to the development of trust and relationship with Mom and Dad. We are building an emotional investment in the future during those early years. The quality of our lifetime relationship with our children is determined by what is accumulated in our family "trust bank."

Some parental styles encourage trust—they allow closeness and attachment to flourish. In time, such styles of parenting build up the trust bank. Other parental styles destroy relationship and deplete the trust bank. Sadly, much "chipping away" is done with the intent of being a good parent. These negative but well-intentioned parents destroy relationship: They distance, embitter, and alienate their children. Such destructive parenting styles can leave a mother wondering why something is missing when she's going through all the supposedly "good-parent hoops." They can distance a child from the very parents he or she needs to love. It's as if a thief is robbing families of the intimate closeness they long for. The thief may be in your home. You may have unwittingly let him in.

Let's Stop Putting the Cart Before the Horse

If so, you are being robbed of the most precious possession you cherish—your own children. Only *you* can protect your family from the thief. You must be willing, however, to start with yourself. It's important that you understand that I'm not talking about child-management but rather, parent-management—"How to get *yourself* to act so your child can trust and stand being with *you*." Let's stop putting the cart before the horse. Let's work at solving family problems by starting with you, the parent.

Will This "Work" in My Family?

I do not offer you the usual guarantees. I do not promise that this will "work" on your children, if by that you mean that they will become more manageable and cherubic. The idea that good parents have perfect children is myth, misinformation. Perfect children should never be the goal of your parenting. So, no, I can't say that your children will change. An emotionally connected parent-child relationship will not guarantee no-problem family living, although it will weather better almost any storm that threatens family life.

I do promise that the suggestions made in the following chapters will work for *you*. You will be focused. You will know the secrets. You will like your parental self better. You may even discover what intrinsic nurturers have known all along: that by meeting your children's needs, by tuning in to the emotional and relational aspects of parenting you may meet the very deepest longings of your own heart.

A key finding in research is that parents of disturbed children give great priority to their own wishes and preferences over those of their children. Parents who get too absorbed in their own goals and wishes are headed for trouble with their kids. If a child feels that his interests are expendable, he feels that he is being treated as an object. He develops mistrust of his parents and begins to doubt the security of his family world.[1]

SEYMOUR AND RHODA FISHER
What We Really Know About Child Rearing

THREE

THE PROBLEM WITH BEING AN "IN YOUR FACE" PARENT:
The Interfering Parent

What parent hasn't looked inward and seen a darkness? Shortly after his first birthday, our firstborn son Brendan dropped napping from his afternoon schedule. I was alarmed. I was certain that something terrible would grow out of this deviation from the normal one-year-old schedule. All my friends' one-year-olds were still taking their afternoon naps. Even the books said he should still be napping. Convinced that one-year-olds need naps (and more convinced that mothers of one-year-olds need their naps), I proceeded to force Brendan into the standard one-year-old developmental mold. After all, "good mothers" make babies take their naps, right?

For five days we engaged in a battle of the wills.

Day 1—I left him alone to cry for long periods of time in his crib. Though the tears flowed, and he fussed and fumed, still, he never wore himself out enough to actually sleep. Worst of all, the dilemma had personal consequences—it was very hard for me to get my nap with Brendan awake and ready to crawl out of his crib and maybe eat roach pills or shave his legs or phone Taiwan. This was not acceptable!

Day 2—Brendan continued to refuse to sleep. How did he do it? How could he be up a couple of times every night and still not need his nap? More important, how could *I* do it? I suspected I was coming down with a serious case of sleep deprivation. All the signs were there—blurry bloodshot eyes, irritability, muscle weakness, extreme fatigue, headache. I was a textbook case. Experiencing withdrawal symptoms, I craved sleep and decided that it was time to become seriously proactive. It was now or never. I marched into his room, 5' 4" of intimidating maternal presence. I grabbed the sides of his bed rail, and delivered a blistering example of "in your face" mothering. Nose to nose, I reprimanded him. With deliberate speech meant to remind him that I was the boss here, I warned the rebel, "THIS IS YOUR NIPPY-NAP TIME. GO—TO—SLEEP!"

His response? He was extremely impressed and scared silly! He sang in his crib!

Day 3—I lost my parental dignity. (Some mothers will do anything to get their sleep.) Still unwilling to surrender my own nap, I brought the little darling to my room. Then I did the only thing I could think of that might work. I closed the communication gap. I put him in bed with me and held his head down. His little eyes would roll to the side to see me. He would smile. Finally he was out of solitary, and Mom had even invented a funny new game to pass the time! What a woman!

Day 4—I escalated the war. I put him back into baby solitary (his crib) and threatened him with bodily harm. He ignored me and with resignation played in his crib. He explored his toe joints and belly button. He passed the time—awake!

Day 5—D-Day! Finally I resorted to my last parental straw. I got out the wooden spanking spoon, declaring, "We need our nippy-naps!" Brendan was spanked that day. *He would just have to learn that one-year-olds need their nippy-naps. He would also have to learn who was in charge around here!* I reasoned.

Oh, I felt better until I looked at his face. I'll never forget his reaction. He looked at me with tears running down his cheeks and simultaneously smiled at me. Adoration was shining through the tears! This was one confused baby! But even though he didn't get it, even though he was in pain, he just had to give me the benefit of the doubt. He just couldn't accept that his darling mother had turned into a crazy, irrational woman! I felt a chill run down my spine. Something was wrong here.

That was seventeen years ago, and with considerable hindsight I would call myself, in those early days of mothering, an "interfering parent." An interfering parent *is tuned out* to the emotional relational aspect of parenting. An interfering parent erodes trust between parent and child.

AN EXAMPLE OF INTERFERENCE

Typically, interfering parents tend to be more aware of what's normal, or what *should be* happening, than they are to their particular child's needs. One attachment theorist observed how this looked in one parent's home where she was observing parent-child bonding. "I watched a mother in the home setting respond to her infant's signals when she had several other demands on her time, with the telephone, housework, and other kids. I saw another mother who was working very hard to put her six-week-old baby on three meals a day—and she was breastfeeding, at that! She would say, 'I don't know why the baby's crying. He was fed at seven o'clock this morning'—it now being after twelve. She would pick him up and play with him very nicely for a while and then put him down, and he would cry again. She would dangle a rattle, she would do this, do that, and she even gave it a bath one day to fill up the time till one o'clock, with the baby off-and-on screaming."[2]

CHARACTERISTICS OF THE INTERFERING STYLE

That mother was operating under the interfering parents' credo, "What *should* be happening!" The baby was telling her what he needed—food! But the interfering parent isn't cued into his or her child's needs. Instead, he or she substitutes adult agendas and desires for flexibility and sensitivity to children's needs.

Besides missing the cues about their children's needs, interfering parents often have an inordinate concern about what other people think about their parenting. They impose on their children a mother-in-law's agendas, a friend's values and structures, or their neighbor's ideas about parenting, with great disregard for their child's individual tendencies and proclivities.

But worst of all, interfering parents turn the parent-child relationship into a power struggle. They tend to be control-oriented. Interfering parents turn nonissues into battlegrounds and die relationally on almost every hill that comes along. All day long they chip away at the trust bank, depleting relational resources and distancing themselves from their children.

THE INSECURELY ATTACHED CHILD

Children learn very soon that they can't trust such a parent; studies show they actually begin to push interfering parents away. Children will exert enormous effort to resist and defend against such adult invasion. Practice the interfering parental style and soon you will see anger, resentment, and yes, great animosity, in your child's eyes.

In her pioneering work in attachment theory, researcher and author Mary Ainsworth has identified this insecurely attached child as the avoidant child. She measures parental interaction with children on a scale called Cooperation and Interference. The cooperative parents fit the child's needs. They relate to the child in a timely manner, when the child is open to them; they don't operate at cross-purposes to the child. The interfering parent gives little attention to the cues from his or her child but does things when the child isn't ready. Interestingly, Ainsworth's research discovered that avoidant babies were held as much as securely attached ones. But interfering mothers of babies who were later avoidant did not hold their children when the baby signaled that it wanted to be held. "So a lot of holding may not help a child to feel secure—unless it is holding that is given when the child signals it needs holding."[3]

SCRIPTURE HAS A WORD FOR *INTERFERENCE*

I'm continually amazed at how applicable Scripture is even to our "cutting edge" knowledge. Scripture has a word for how the interfering parents affect their children. It's called *exasperation*. "Fathers," Ephesians 6:4 warns, "do not exasperate your children." In other words, don't irritate, don't nag, don't "catastrophize," don't pester, don't smother, don't interfere, don't control! Essentially—back off!

Three Big Battlegrounds: Eating, Dressing, and Bedtime

One friend told this story about her three-year-old. Like me, in retrospect, she could laugh at the absurdity of her behavior. It seems she had been having trouble getting her daughter to eat at mealtime. Food was left untouched meal after meal. Wanting to be a good mother who oversees her child's nutrition and health, my friend became desperate enough to resort to some humiliating tactics. While her daughter was distracted, watching TV, my friend would sneak quietly into the room, trying not to be seen, and would try to stuff healthy food into her daughter's mouth. It didn't work! Frustrated at the continual interruption, the little girl would yell, "No!" and push her mother away. More and more this had become a patterned response to her mother even when food wasn't involved.

But, aren't we supposed to *make* our children eat healthy food? Isn't that part of being a good parent?

The amazing thing is that children *will* eat when they are hungry. They will not starve themselves. Typically, eating becomes an issue only when some well-meaning adult turns it into a power struggle. Many parents regard mealtimes as opportunities to impose their authority on their children. Instead of a highly delightful and relational hour, we adults manage to transform one of the most natural things in the world—eating—into a battleground. The parent-child relationship should never be stressed out over such a nonessential hill. Once moms and dads learn to ask, "What is my child telling me he or she needs?" (space, not such a quantity of food, and so forth) then we will take the cues and back off the controls. Once my friend backed away from the controls, her daughter's appetite reappeared and she wasn't greeted with, "No! No!" every time she entered her daughter's room.

Solution? Let the child be.

I once heard a fellow teacher explain her philosophy on child-rearing. It seems that she felt that her children should be well-dressed and clean at all times so at a second's notice she could take them out in public and not be embarrassed by their appearance. In her thinking, that's what good parents do. Good mothers have well-groomed, well-taken-care-of kids, adult in every way except for their size. Right? *Wrong!*

I felt so sorry for her kids. I can't imagine childhood without muddy shoes and a hole to dig in, hair that's mussed and no one loves you any less. What a burden! Imagine having to look good at all times for your mother's public image. (Remember: Interfering parents often care inordinately about what other people think about their parental image.)

Solution? Someone should take those poor little sanitized kids and roll them in the mud for an afternoon! They would love it! There's more to the parent-child relationship than policing children in the clean-and-pressed department. If cleanliness is based on our own parental image, then we need to reexamine our motives. It's hardly the issue over which to sacrifice our parental-child relationship.

Another woman described how stressful bedtime had become at their house. It seems that all the emotional fuss was over whether her five-year-old could wear his street clothes to bed. Mom, wanting to be a good mom, had drawn the line and insisted on a bath and jammies every night. So every night in tears, and with considerable threats and yelling from Mom, her son was put to bed, a miserable but clean child.

Someday that young mom will wish she had a picture of those dirty little feet sticking out from under the sheets. Someday, that will seem incredibly adorable. Moms think they always need clean kids in clean jammies in clean sheets, but sometimes what kids need is just to drop exhausted into bed whether they're clean or not. Try it! Your kids will love you for it!

Oh, the things we do to our children in the name of good parenting!

GOOD NEWS! RELAX!

Solution? Relax. That's the very good news about being a good parent. We can relax about many of the nonessentials. Don't worry about what your neighbors, or your mother-in-law, or your best friend may think. Go ahead—let him occasionally sleep in his street clothes, his undies, or his Halloween costume. It really doesn't matter that much. If your little girl's idea of mealtime variety is the different ways you can cut a peanut butter sandwich, so what? Someday that peanut-butter lover will be off at college, living on salads and granola bars! When she's gone, you may long for the days when that little face was smeared with peanut butter and jelly.

Children can be so charmingly eccentric. It's part of their appeal. If we adults could just learn to loosen up enough to enjoy and appreciate that aspect of childhood!

TUNING IN TO THE RIGHT QUESTION

What am I saying? I'm saying that nurturing parents learn to ask, not just, "Why is this kid acting this way?" or "How can I get my child to do it my way?" but "What does this child really *need*?"

A "tuned-in" parent understands that bedtime should not be turned into a battleground. It is much more important that a child be sent to bed happily and securely than that bedtime is strictly enforced to the second on the clock. A child who experiences bedtime trauma, complete with heavy crying, threats, or spankings every night, is experiencing something more. He or she is experiencing relational injury with his or her parents. Every night chips away at the trust bank and reinforces a growing emotional gap. Every night, bedtime inflexibility creates bedtime histrionics that destroy the relational bond.

A "tuned-in" parent knows that the clock is secondary to the emotional relational issues of security and comfort. Those are the *real* bedtime issues. So what, if the child-management books say that nine o'clock is the appropriate bedtime for school nights? Look at your own child's physical and emotional needs. If you're getting him up at six A.M. for child care, he or she may need to go to bed even earlier than nine P.M. Make sure you are not choosing a rigid time based on what *you* want. Child management is not the *primary* goal of your parenting.

A REVEALING CONVERSATION

A young mom good-naturedly challenged me on this after a seminar I gave recently. I had shared how, not being much of a night person, I have usually been in bed before my grade school children. When they were tired, they went to bed. The young mom was incredulous. My solutions sounded too simple to her. "Every night is a major battle at our house. But I just can't believe that the problem could be solved if I backed off like you say!"

"What time is bedtime at your house?" I queried.

"Oh, we start about eight o'clock."

"What terrible things do you think would happen if you backed off the strict bedtime?"

"Well, I think they would really take advantage of the situation. They'd probably stay up to watch David Letterman, for pete's sake!"

"Okay. (It was a possibility, I had to admit.) You're saying that that's one issue you just can't back away from. Then let's see if you can back off from the controls somewhere else. Tell me what mealtimes are like at your house."

"They're terrible! The kids fight and fuss about what I fix. We've considered eating in shifts so they don't eat together at the table."

"What do they fight over?"

"Everything."

"Do you think you could just back off a little on the controls at mealtime?"

"Oh, I couldn't do that. They would never eat right or learn any decent manners. Impossible."

I walked that young mother through her entire day with her children. There was not one area in which she was willing to relax. Her home was a battleground all day long. All day long she was chipping away at the relationship she was supposed to be building with her children.

Besides, the strangest thing of all, she thought that her children were responsible for all the wars in her home—that *they* were impossible. For the first time in her parental life she began to see how *she* was the major contributor to family strife and ill-will. She was the responsible one, not her children.

ALIGN YOUR PASSIONS AND PICK YOUR BATTLES!

Every parent does and should have some areas in which he or she lays down rules and stands firm. Truly interfering parents, however, aren't interfering in just a few areas. They aren't selective about it. They're simply interfering, exasperating, nagging parents all day long, on every issue that raises its head.

They sacrifice their children to peas and carrots, brushing and flossing, picking up and staying neat, and a thousand other nonessential issues.

> There is room for passion in family life, but it must be passion for people. If we care deeply about anything, it must be for the ones in our care. We must guard against anything that would threaten healthy family relationships.

How displaced our passions can become! In some homes an altar of the heart is being built. It is an altar of sacrifice that requires the relationships of the ones you love. Care passionately about anything other than your children, make war over things and how they're cared for, alienate everyone you are supposed to be loving, and you might as well go ahead and lay your children on that altar of your unfaithful heart. In time, if not sooner, you will lose them.

There is room for passion in family life, but it must be passion for people. If we care deeply about anything, it must be for the ones in our care. We must guard against anything that would threaten healthy family relationships.

FOCUS!

Ask the primary question: "What does my child need?" The answer is not necessarily clean pillowcases, vegetables, and proper bedtimes. The answer is: Our children need us to be the guardians of the trust, the protectors of family relationships, parents with clear focus, and pure hearts. They need us to have faithful hearts—to care deeply, passionately, and affectionately for them.

We are not uncaring. In fact, we interfere precisely because we *do* care. God, help us to simply care about the right things—our families, our children, our spouses. God, help us to refocus and earn back the trust we've destroyed. God, help us to be the parents You intended us to be.

FOUR

HOW TO KEEP DISPLACED PASSIONS FROM DESTROYING YOUR FAMILY LIFE:

The Intentional Parent

I can still see her in my mind. There was something vulnerable or fragile about her. At first glance I thought she was beautiful, but as we talked, I realized that her body language communicated brittleness, too. With her arms held close to her sides, her straight back, and guarded face, she gave off an up-tight aura, as if she were slightly uncomfortable in her own skin. From her matching heels to her "every hair in place" grooming, she was put together but not at ease.

She only said a few sentences to me, but they contained a world of discouragement and disappointment, mostly directed at herself.

"I'm not very good with people. I just don't seem to relate. My parents were very strict. I could never please them. Now I've got four children of my own. I'm home schooling them, and I'm turning out just like my own parents. I'm 'in their face' all day long. I just don't seem to be able to stop myself."

She is an interfering parent.

I wish I could give this young mother a quick fix, a pill that would help her relax and enjoy life more, but changing relational patterns is like many other things in life: It's a process, not a quick zap. What are parents to do when they sense they are the cause for the break in relationship at home with their children? How can we help ourselves to be less "in their faces" and more "in their hearts"?

A PLAN FOR INTENTIONAL PARENTING

We need to move away from the interfering parental style to what I call an *intentional parenting* style. It's a plan, a system, to help redirect and clarify our parental goal.

Why do you need a plan? Because developing a healthy parental style, one that is highly relational and freed up to meet your children's real needs, requires shifting from an automatic approach to a more thought-through, self-disciplined method.

Let me explain. If you found out you were overextended in your personal finances and you sought help, the first thing the experts would do would be to come up with a plan, a system, a budget to help you get back in control of your finances.

If you had a weight problem, you might use a diet system, or a lifestyle eating program that would help you lose weight and overcome poor eating habits.

You know that wanting to be financially responsible, or to be thin, are not enough to get you to your goal. Otherwise we would all be rich and thin!

So it is with wanting to be a relational parent. It is not enough to recognize its importance or even to desire it intensely. You will need a system to hang those longings on—something that brings about real change.

HOW TO DETERMINE YOUR FAMILY VALUES

You will need to learn how to distinguish between issues that are truly important in your children's development and those that are secondary. You will need to think through your values and family priorities to come up with a clear, precise, communicable system that works. If it seems like more work than you've had to do in your parenting before, let me encourage you to apply yourself to this task. The result? You will be able to relax and enjoy your children more.

So how does a parent discern between issues deserving priority attention and those that should be backed away from? You will need to make a decision based upon the questions: *What issues are life-forming and therefore consequential for your children's future life? Which issues are not consequential for their future life?*

Perhaps that is what is implied in Scripture when parents are instructed to "Train up their children in the way they should go." In other words, look to the future, Mom, Dad. What will they need to know, what skills should they be developing for that journey into the future?

You decide the important issues; these become nonnegotiables. Many interfering parents exasperate their children by having too many nonnegotiables. These children, like the young mother at the beginning of this chapter, view their parents as "strict" and impossible to please. Many children, in exasperation, give up trying to please. Their parents have failed to differentiate between the real and nonissues, and so often these children fail to differentiate as well. No one has ever helped them prioritize life values.

I've found it's a great help to have no more than five or six nonnegotiable areas that are clearly communicated to our children as our most important values. What's most amazing, I've come to learn, is that it really doesn't matter which particular five you pick, just so you keep them to basic values and clearly communicate them to your children.

THE PRIORITIES IN THE BELL HOME

What do the five nonnegotiables look like at the Bell house? What areas do we think are consequential to our children's future lives? What do we get passionate about in our family?

Here they are. Remember, they may be very different from the ones you might establish, and that's okay. I am not suggesting that your family needs to resemble ours. This is just a model to show you the kinds of things you might pick.

1. Obedience Is Important.

Once children understand how you interpret obedience, you can avoid a lot of the wear and tear. From their earliest days we've explained to our kids what this means. The message is strong: Don't directly disobey us, unless you want to suffer the consequences. Also, after you've been told no, don't whine and nag, trying to wear us down. That's disobedience, too! If something you've been asked to do seems unreasonable, find ways to respectfully appeal. We can be flexible. We have occasionally changed our minds when the appeal has been rational and reasonable (*never* if the appeal is whiney, angry, or tearful). Most of the time, it means staying within the prescribed boundaries. Steve and I are trying to prepare our two sons for the future day when they will have a boss who will have power over their lives. They will need to know how to get along with authority figures.

2. Mutual Respect Is Absolutely Essential.

I wouldn't think of sending my children into their future with "attitudes." I recently spent an excruciating afternoon with a mother and daughter. The girl constantly interrupted our conversation, corrected her mother, and made herself (with the force of a fourteen-year-old terrorist, I might add) the center of our adult attentions. She absolutely bullied us. I felt guilty thinking it, but she was the most obnoxious child I've ever had to spend an afternoon with. Why didn't her mother teach her some basic, gracious social skills? Why did this mother take such childish harassment? This happens to be my own hot button, my own pet peeve, that you may not feel is very important. You may be able to relax more at this point than I can. My own sense is that my children need to be taught not to correct us (publicly), or to interrupt our conversations, including telephone conversations (unless it's important, and then the key, the open-sesame to the adult conversational door, is a polite "Excuse me," until they are recognized).

We also try to operate within the boundaries of mutual respect. We believe, in other words, that respect is not a rule applied just in the way our children relate to us but in the way we relate to them and in the way they are allowed to relate to one another. I question some experts' opinions that sibling rivalry is a natural, normal process that parents should best stay out of. Too many adults end up in years of therapy because of the way a sibling was allowed to treat them in their growing-up years.

In our situation particularly, raising two boys, I want them to understand what it means to be sensitive to other people's feelings. Someday they will be responsible for their own families. We're training them now to be the caring, loving fathers and husbands we hope they will become. We're training them now to be each other's closest allies, perhaps even best friends. Our hope here is that if you can learn to be nice even to your brother, you will have developed a life skill of graciousness toward other people, too. (I have to report a conversation I overheard recently: A younger boy was talking in the back seat of our car to our youngest son, Justin. The boy said, "Is your brother a big jerk to you? Is he mean to you?" I was so thrilled to hear Justin answer that question with, "No, he's not mean to me—he's really my best friend!")

3. Excellence Is the Standard.

This means that homework is important and worth doing well. In our work we try to give it our best.

I know some families who go even further and state that homework must be done before anything else. We really don't say that. We say that it has to be done—and done well. They can blow the rest of the afternoon when they get home from school. My kids need that break. But in the evening, before TV, sports activities, or church youth group, before talking on the phone, the homework has to be completed.

Why is excellence important? Because someday they will enter the workforce and have a job to do. It will need to be done well and fit into their lives as a priority. Much of their accomplishment and success in life begins with the habits they develop during their student years. It's extremely consequential for their future life, so it's important in our home!

Again, what a heavy burden this value would be if it were directed only at our children. Steve and I try to model a "job well done," too. We think it's important not to have a double standard for parents and children in this area. So ALL the Bells try to do their best work.

4. We are a community of faith. We participate in the spiritual life of the home and church.

We all attend church. Our boys also attend weekly youth activities. They participate in small groups (as do their parents). They have prayer partners. (So do we.) They avail themselves of the life of the church, participating in Bible studies, weekend retreats, camps with a spiritual emphasis, and so on.

We're convinced as parents that we need the help of other believers to raise our children. Brendan and Justin need the church to help nurture Christian friendships and a maturing faith.

We also participate in spiritual life together as a family. Our usual thirty-minute ride home from church is typically spent discussing and applying the sermon. We pray at mealtimes and often at bedtime, or whenever requested. We make it a practice to share our struggles with one another and look to God for strength and wisdom to deal with our lives.

Finally, I'm aware that our last nonnegotiable may surprise you.

5. Piano lessons and practicing are a must!

Not only is piano practicing considered an essential at the Bell home, but it's also a relational hill I've chosen to die on nearly every day for the past six or seven years. (However, I try to die as unemotionally as possible. I resist the urge to hyperventilate or turn red from screaming. I try not to emote. But I do know that a certain younger son would love it if his mother and father would rethink this one.)

Why piano? Because God gave Justin some musical talent. By that, I don't mean that we think he's a prodigy. But, it's something that he has a gift in. However, without discipline and hard work this natural bent will not mature beyond "Chopsticks." To play well, he will have to work. Solitary hours spent bent over the keyboard, working out finger-ing, phrasing, and dynamics over and over teaches culture—something, frankly, that sports cannot offer. We want our children eventually to be able to play, at least for their own enjoyment. Also, we want our boys, when they hear a performance by someone else, to understand the hard work and sacrifice that went into the creation of that kind of beauty.

As I said, your particular list of nonnegotiables will probably be different from ours. It will be determined by your own family values and the needs of your children.

ARE YOU COMMUNICATING YOUR REAL VALUES TO YOUR CHILDREN?

While working on this chapter, I thought it would be interest-ing to ask each of our boys individually what they thought the five non-negotiables were in our home. I wanted to see if we had actually com-municated our values to our kids. I realized that we had never articulated them as one, two, three, four, five, so I was curious to test my theory. Would they be able to verbalize them? Had we communicated our val-ues? We were encouraged and a bit surprised. They got them all—not word for word but principle by principle—they had the basic ideas.

Many of their sentences started with words like, "Mom, you would have our necks if . . ." or "Dad, you would really be mad if . . ." While this may not exactly sound complimentary, it is an identification of the passion with which we communicate. Passion has a place if it is attached to a real parental value. One by one our sons described their parents' boundaries. "If we ever disobeyed you, it would be nasty around here. You don't ever let us forget. You say that's passive resistance. If our grades were low, you'd be on us like a 'flea on a dog' (one of my favorite descriptions of what can happen to our relationship if *they* break the trust—a parent monitoring their every move is the last thing they want!). You would probably ground us for life if we ever talked back to you! Church is important to you. And, of course, there's always the piano, waiting for us at the end of every day. We'd say that if we really wanted to pick a fight with our parents, we'd know exactly how to do it!"

"Brendan," I probed curiously, "you see how a lot of other families operate. From what you've seen in your friends' homes, how would you characterize your own parents? Are we strict or lenient?"

His answer was interesting. I thought being invited to compare us to other parents might be seen as an opportunity to tell us that we were the strictest parents he had ever seen! He surprised me.

"Well, actually, I would say you're both. You don't get upset about a lot of stuff, but the stuff you and Dad really care about—watch out!"

Exactly! This son not only knows his parents, he knows their values as well. He knows our values by the things we get passionate about.

THE VALUES OF A PRESIDENT'S MOTHER

I noted when President George Bush's mother died in early 1993, during the last days of his presidency, that he chose to describe her in terms of her values—values that were almost paradoxically very loving but also strict.

Mr. Bush said about her, "Every mother has her own style. My mother's was a little like an army drill sergeant's. Dad was the commanding general, make no mistake about that, but Mother was the one out there day in and day out, shaping the troops. They believed in an old-fashioned way of bringing up the family—generous measures of both love and discipline."

George Bush's mother instilled her values in her children. She encouraged participation in athletics. Church attendance was strictly enforced. President Bush recalled that "each morning as we gathered at the breakfast table, Mother or Dad read a Bible lesson to us."

Many of her values would be reflected in her son. She valued volunteerism. She also emphasized graciousness—something even Bush's political critics would admit was one of his strong points. As a young man, Mr. Bush remembered, when he came home with stories of his exploits in sports, she would listen and then ask, "George, were there other boys playing on the team?" Years later, while serving in the White

House, after he had delivered one of his speeches, she warned him, "You're talking too much about yourself, George."[1]

What a wonderful heritage! Does anyone really care that she never got George to eat broccoli? No! Are we glad she concentrated on the essentials that helped establish a president's character? Yes!

From what he's described, I'd project that the family values of the home where George Bush grew up were as follows:

1. Spiritual life
2. Service to your fellow man
3. Humility
4. Graciousness
5. Discipline (I suspect that sports were to Mrs. Bush what piano practicing is to Valerie Bell.)

"YOUR PARENTS ARE RELIGIOUS AND STRICT, AREN'T THEY?"

Whatever your values, it's important to understand: It's possible to be a disciplined parent without coming across to your children as overly strict and relationally severe.

Our youngest reported a conversation with a teacher that probably left her feeling a little confused. She said, "You Bell boys seem to be turning out all right—your parents must be very strict."

Justin answered, "No, not really. They're not even as strict as a lot of my friends' parents."

Then the teacher's response that followed made all of us laugh when we heard it, "But they make you go to church, don't they?"

"Yes," my son replied, "but that doesn't make them strict!"

Don't you love it? Isn't it a hopeful sign when our children defend the truth that parents with religious values can also be highly relational parents as well? It's a myth that "religious" parents are always rigid, cold, overly strict disciplinarians! Just ask Justin, he'll set the record straight!

WHERE YOUR PASSIONS ARE, THERE WILL YOUR VALUES BE

So how do you go about establishing a relational yet principled home? Well, first realize that several factors will determine your family values. The first factor relates to what you get passionate about. It will accomplish nothing to establish values you think you *should* have, when in actuality, you get passionate about other things. Interestingly, children—ours, yours—always know what parents *really* care about. As an experiment, I asked several families with intact, solid Christian homes to list their family values. To find out if the children perceived their parents' values, I suggested they create two separate lists. One the parents would write; the other would be the nonnegotiables as viewed by the children. One highly relational family received this list from their children:

1. Obey our parents.
2. Take care of things we own (pets, pick up belongings, and so forth).
3. Piano.
4. Get approval before making plans for activities.
5. Family night is a priority. (This is the one night a week when they have family devotions and time for connecting spiritually.)

The mother was surprised about the second point—"Take care of the things we own." She hadn't consciously made it a passion point, but the more she thought about it, she realized that she often said things like, "Mother doesn't want to be your servant. I am not your slave," and so forth. One thing is absolutely sure: Children will always pick up on our *real* values. We can say we care about reading—but if the TV is always on—our children soon realize that we don't *really* care that much about reading. By our passion levels we convey our real values to our children.

If your passions are displaced, you will end up with a number of nonessential things on your family values list—and in time any rational child will "buy out" of foolish standards instead of "buy in." Frankly, some of us parents are in need of a passion-adjustment. We need to stop being passionate about the piddly! Be passionate about the things that will have an impact on your child's character and future.

Another factor that will determine your list of nonnegotiable values is the age of your children. Your list must be age-appropriate. For instance, Brendan, when he turned sixteen, convinced us that he had learned all he would learn from piano lessons, so his fifth point was changed to always letting us know where he is at ten-thirty at night if he's not home yet. This is a shift to a more age-appropriate value. Therefore, you may find it necessary to make a few adjustments through the years as your children mature.

SOME OTHER FAMILIES' VALUES

This is the list from another highly relational home where there are several small children. Some of the children are preschool and the others are early grade school. So these are the years before there is much homework or piano lessons. Incidentally, just as the Bell values are influenced by Mom and Dad's being musicians, this list is influenced by the fact that Dad is a medical doctor (see point 5).

1. Honor Christ.
2. Treat others as you want to be treated.
3. Be respectful and have good manners. (The mother and father in this home are both very gracious people.)
4. Be disciplined with your work. Work hard when you work. Play hard when you play.
5. Safety rules. (There are boundaries about where to ride their bikes. They are warned not to take pills or medicine they may find around the house. They are warned not to speak to strangers, or let anyone touch them in places that are covered when they wear swimming suits.)

Obviously, this fifth rule grows out of Dad's frequently having to treat children in emergency rooms, as well as a sense of age-appropriateness for the many small children in their family.

A business executive (CEO of a large manufacturing company with offices around the world) and his wife identified these five family-value areas. They have four children, who range in age from early grade school to high school.

1. Obedience is expected.
2. TV viewing is limited.
3. Integrity and honesty are important.
4. Respect is practiced toward all family members.
5. Bad language is not acceptable.

It's interesting that this executive and his company are known for their integrity and for taking the high road in the business world.

Obviously, the values of the father are being passed down to his children because he sees how important they are to success in the real world, as seen through his "business" grid.

IT'S A MATTER OF CLEAR FOCUS

We do transmit our passions to our children. We should never waste our parental passion on the piddly! If you are a nutritionist, then eating healthy food will probably be extremely important to you. Chances are that this will be one of your five family values. It's not on my list, but that's okay—probably piano practicing isn't on yours! My point: Limit your passion areas to five, and clearly communicate them within your family. Be sure to align your passion with the areas you feel are truly important. This very focused approach in relating who we are and the things we value to our children is the process I'm calling *Becoming Intentional*. The intentional-parenting style stands in direct contrast to the haphazard, relationally destructive approach of the interfering-parental style.

One area that is often mentioned when I talk to parents about their values is TV-watching. Many families feel the need to limit viewing time and the type of programming their children are exposed to. I have no problem with that.

It simply hasn't been much of a problem in our home (because when doing all your homework, and attending all those youth meetings, and practicing that piano—I mean, a kid only has so many hours in a day!) Occasionally, it has been an issue, but it's just never been enough of an issue to make our top-five list.

WHAT ABOUT OTHER AREAS NOT IN THE TOP FIVE?

So what do we do about TV guidelines in our home? Or put more broadly, after you've picked your five family values, what happens about all the other important but maybe not life-forming areas? Do you simply ignore those areas?

This a very important question, and the answer is key to becoming a relational but principled parent. Answer: You back off but not entirely. You consistently teach about them. You talk about them. But you do not go to war over them. Let me explain. By "going to war," I mean escalating the emotional tone when "instructing." You choose not to communicate with too much passion or intensity regarding these issues. You may even choose to pass over them occasionally. Above all, you don't turn the parent-child relationship into a disaster by interfering about those lesser areas.

BUT MY KIDS ARE ALL SO DIFFERENT!

Occasionally it may be necessary to customize the list for a child's individual needs. If a child is struggling and failing in an important area (let's take honesty, for example) and it's not on your list, but you know that this child will suffer miserable consequences in life if this weak area isn't addressed, then customize the list for a while until you sense that progress has been made.

HOW CAN I MAKE A CHANGE AFTER ALL THESE YEARS?

What if you are midstream in your parenting and you are going to try to distill your values into five main areas? What's the best approach? I suggest that you sit down with your children and come to a consensus about what you value as a family. Include your children, because the children are much more apt to "buy in" or have ownership in the process if they are included. You will be more likely to work as a family team when it comes to applying your values if you've agreed on most of them together.

For years I was a grade-school music teacher. Usually I traveled from classroom to classroom. This was a wonderful environment for studying differing approaches of classroom teachers to working with children. Through the years, I observed that the most effective teachers had several things in common. Their classroom rules were clearly communicated, often written and displayed publicly. The rules were few. Often the rules were the result of the children's own input. Finally, the rules were consistently enforced. It was a formula for smooth-running classrooms. It also works at home!

EARNING THE RIGHT TO BE HEARD

Every once in a while, a concern will arise wherein a parent will wonder: Is this something that should be an issue? Maybe it's not on "the list," but it seems important, just the same. For instance, one evening we were sitting around a meal with friends when such a topic came up. Their daughter was starting to date and was getting more serious with a man whom the parents considered an inappropriate match. They had observed some rather alarming characteristics in this young man. He was controlling, had a flashing temper, and was financially irresponsible. In their opinion, he was a disaster waiting to happen.

We discussed whether it was appropriate or wise to "go to war" and confront their daughter about the potential disaster of becoming involved with this young man. We batted back and forth the pros and cons of direct opposition to their relationship. The potential of driving them closer together was real as was the possibility of damaging their relationship with their daughter. The adults came to no consensus. Then the father turned to Brendan, our seventeen-year-old, and asked, "Brendan, you're a kid. What do you think we should do?"

Well, this should be good! I silently gasped. *What does a seventeen-year-old know about such things?*

"Oh, yes, you should say something, definitely!" Brendan replied instantly.

I believe Brendan was right. A parent may find himself needing to be an interfering parent! When? *When the issue has future drastic impact on your child!*

> There is an even more compelling reason to strengthen the family through relationship: There is clear evidence that from the strength and health of the family comes a child's ability to withstand destructive behaviors such as drug and alcohol abuse, sexual promiscuity, and other self-destructive conduct.

But . . . a word of caution here. You will never get away with such blatant opposition if you have already depleted the family trust bank on trivia. How your intervention is perceived is determined by the strength of your relationship. Sometimes, to help our children avoid disaster, we need to be parental and get out all the parental ammunition we have. We will not have "earned the right to be heard" if we've depleted our family relationships with trivial passions, if our children perceive us as being controlling and manipulatively self-serving. A family trust bank with daily investments through the years can withstand a huge withdrawal, if need be, and still have a reserve of trust.

There is an even more compelling reason to strengthen the family through relationship: There is clear evidence that from the strength and health of the family comes a child's ability to withstand destructive behaviors such as drug and alcohol abuse, sexual promiscuity, and other self-destructive conduct. That is why so much of the mental-health-care system is emphasizing family therapy—to help troubled children and teenagers by *first* strengthening the family system. The simple truth is that a child from a healthy system has a much better chance of succeeding in life, of avoiding destructive life choices, and developing to his or her potential.

Bottom line: The interfering trust-breaking parent tries to build family through too many controls. The intentional trust-building parent strengthens family through value clarification and trustworthy relationships. The interfering parent practices bond-breaking, while the intentional parent builds a strong parent-child attachment.

It is a fortunate child whose parents understand and practice the difference.

PART TWO:

...And
Into Their Hearts

. . . here I stand, not only with the sense
Of present pleasure, but with pleasing thoughts
That in this moment there is life and food
For future years.

WILLIAM WORDSWORTH
Tintern Abbey

FIVE
YOU ARE THE MEMORY:
Parents Who Wound,
Parents Who Sustain

We had a high school graduation party at our house last June. Our son thought we made too big a deal of it, but as parents we saw it differently. When a child graduates from high school, it's a life passage—one that turns most parents into sentimental slobs. I know. Against my better judgment, it made me subject our adult friends to our son's baby movies. Politely, and with the patience usually reserved for those becoming somewhat senile, they accompanied me on my public sentimental journey. We all agreed he was adorable!

He sang into a make-believe microphone, he stuffed M&Ms into his brother's mouth, he blew kisses, he ran with a waddle—he was, in retrospect, precious. Occasionally the camera caught a glimpse of a haggard-looking young mother—tired and slightly unkempt—no match for this energized automaton of a two-year-old.

And then a friend said, "Don't you wish you could somehow get back into that picture and hug him one more time?" She spoke the impossible wish of every parental heart. Don't you wish . . . ?

I remembered what the camera couldn't capture—what my guests couldn't see—my feelings of ambivalence toward my child back then. I had never anticipated feeling anything but love for my child, so I was frightened to find my heart occasionally cool, distant, perfunctory. I hadn't counted on this! Once I even hesitantly revealed to an older woman that I felt as though I were living with a terrorist! It was a dark, frightening admission— sometimes I did not feel loving toward my own child.

"I am having trouble loving my son. He makes me so angry!" The words filled me with shame.

This experienced mother, who had successfully maneuvered four children of her own through the "terrible twos," laughed and said, "Valerie, that's why God had to make two-year-olds so cute! Otherwise they would all be killed by their own parents!"

How did she know how out-of-control this child could make me feel?

And then she tossed me this insight: "But, look at it this way— if *you* don't love him, nobody will. And if *you* don't love him—he will die!"

In the days and weeks ahead I remembered those words—*If you don't love him—he will die!* I knew the words were true. A parent is the food and sustenance of a child's emotional development. What happens today between parent and child matters tomorrow and twenty years from now. I loved my child! I wanted to give him everything I could. I set my heart to the sacrificial, energy-consuming, life-draining task of loving him. I became aware that I was not simply giving him hugs, forgiving his "babyness," taking care of him, being patient, and so forth, and getting through the day, but that I was giving him in these pleasant moments the life and food for future years—the ingredients that would form his emotional health.

THE PARENT IS PRIMARY

Like many parents, my attitude was the problem. My child was not at fault. I needed help to parent well. Healthy children begin with healthy parents. Any approach to family that starts by focusing on the child is putting the cart before the horse. Additionally, families can only be as healthy as the parents. Individual family members may be healthier than the parents, but the family system will only be as healthy as the parents who lead it. That's why we must focus on the health of parents instead of simply the management of the child. *You* are extremely important. *You* matter today and tomorrow. *You* are *primary*.

PARENTS WHO ARE IN THE CLOUDS ABOUT THEIR ROLE

Parents who underestimate their impact on their children remind me of a man who planned to play a joke on his neighbors. Taking a lawn chair from his garage, he anchored it with ropes to stakes in his backyard. Then he attached weather balloons to the four corners and filled them with hot air. Eagerly he imagined his neighbors' surprised faces as he hovered over their yards in his homemade aircraft. What a great prank! The rascal could almost hear the laughs his little escapade would provide. Undoubtedly he would become the stuff of neighborhood legend!

Then, with the balloons snapping to attention over his head, he executed the last step of his plan. With confidence and delight in his own creativity, he sat down and untied the rope anchors. It worked! To his delight he felt himself rising, but it soon became obvious that this was no hover craft! Before he could yell, "Hi, how ya'll doin'? Just thought I'd drop in for a bit!" to his neighbors, before he could wave to the crowds from his one-man parade, he found himself rising into the atmosphere at an alarming speed.

He had not planned on how to pilot his craft! Up into the atmosphere he rose until he was just a spot in the distance—an unintentional UFO—if he was noticed at all from the earth below.

I suppose I heard of how this neighborhood jokester was rescued, but unfortunately I don't remember! No matter. He serves the purpose for my illustration even if we leave him dangling in the clouds, with only an occasional glimpse of the soles of his shoes.

That's because I'm convinced that too many parents are like our startled astronaut! They plan their family years with the best of intentions. Laughter and love fill the homes of their imaginations. They birth and raise their children with devotion. Through the years they sacrifice and do without so that children can have music lessons, camp, and college.

But there comes a moment when they realize that their well-intentioned plans have gone awry. Maybe it's their child's look of disdain, or an explosion of angry hateful words, or a child who goes to great lengths to avoid being with them—the hurtful wound can be delivered in so many ways.

And like our astonished aviator, the change seems so sudden. How did all this emotional distance happen? When did the relational gap grow so wide? Talk to mothers and fathers, and you will soon realize that the family stratosphere is heavily trafficked with parents who are hurting and wondering what happened. There they dangle, just like our over-the-fence prankster, full of grief and unanswered questions.

What went wrong?

Why is my child so angry?

Why have we become so distant from each other?

For the balloon man and many puzzled parents, the answer to their problem is the same. The problem is all that hot air! If they want to close the distance, if they want to survive, then they're going to have to get rid of some of that hot air! Their children cannot do it. Their spouse cannot do it. They must take responsibility for the emotional tone of their home. They must begin with themselves.

I'm sure our prankster-inventor eventually figured it out, but is it so obvious to most parents?

THE UNSAFE PARENT; WHEN YOUR CHILDREN ARE NOT YOUR PRIORITY

I watched a TV talk show recently and observed the dynamics between a shriveled-up old man and his middle-aged son. Before the national audience, the son accused: "You never ask how my job's going! When I come home to visit, you just want to take me down to the VFW hall and show me off to your buddies. But when we get back to your house, you just plunk yourself in front of your TV and hardly even talk to me! When you visit my home, you criticize how we do things—you don't like the food my wife cooks, or the way we raise the kids! You're impossible!"

The son's angry words are flowing at projectile speed now. He's emotionally vomiting. It seems the litany of provocations is never-ending. In various ways the son says, "We aren't connecting, there is no relationship here! And I am angry as I can be about it!"

The wizened father seems to shrink further before our eyes. He weakly protests. He tries to explain that these things, although they are true, do not mean that he doesn't love his son. He defends his attitudes and actions. "Hot air!"

The old man exhibits an unbelievable denseness. He just refuses to "get it"! He would not move from his intractable viewpoint even to concede, "Son, I understand that's how you feel." Talk about talking to a brick wall!

If he doesn't want to understand why his son is so angry, why has he subjected himself to this humiliating public pillory? The process is obviously painful to him. My guess is that he wouldn't be here if he didn't care for his son, but he wants something more than he wants relationship with his son. He has an agenda that won't allow him to hear his son's pain.

More than anything, he wants to win the fight. That's the most important thing! He wants to be right!

That day the gap would not be closed by even one small degree. The "experts" are mired down in the nuances. The old man and his son are holding their ground. I turn the TV off, frustrated for both of them.

I know how they got where they are. Interfering parenting! The trust bank has been chipped away at and now only anger and resentment are left behind. The parents are relationally and emotionally bankrupt!

Parents who want to win at any cost, who refuse to understand how a child feels (regardless of how irrational those feelings may appear), who exhibit unbelievable denseness even in the face of a child's great emotional pain are emotionally unsafe parents. Eventually they bankrupt the parent-child relationship. As the talk show demonstrated, even into their adult years, children of unsafe parents continue to hurt from their negative impact.

A LIFE SENTENCE

Let me describe the interaction I observed recently between another unsafe parent and her children. She sat next to me in the waiting room of a beauty parlor. It was a place where you could get a haircut for ten bucks. We were all looking for a bargain. The mother had brought her children with her. They were driving her crazy. Hands on mother, hands on glass. Running, yelling, whooping it up—they were boisterous and beyond control. What a show they put on! There was no way that I or the other customers could ignore her children. But the eyes really began to roll when Mom began to lose it.

"Sit down and shut up!" she blasted. "Stop it! I'm going to take you home and make you take a nap right now if you don't stop it!" (Good idea! We'll try not to miss you, the exchanged glances of the other customers communicated.)

"If you touch me one more time, I'll never take you anywhere again! You're such a brat! I'm going to dump you at Grandma's house and leave you there!"

But strangely, her children didn't seem intimidated by her bullying posture. What was this? Had they at their young ages already developed a childhood immunity to her, a kind of callus over the usual child-sensitivity? In fact, it was odd, but instead of registering woundedness, I got the impression that her kids had learned to cope by playing a "Let's-drive-mother-even-more-crazy" game!

For the next ten minutes she berated and screamed at her children in a break-the-sound-barrier voice. They continued to think of ways to annoy her (and everyone in the place).

Finally her dark curly-haired, about-three-years-old son had had enough. He said what many of us were thinking. Turning to her, he pointed a stubby baby finger and yelled, "YOU'RE FIRED!"

I almost laughed out loud! And then my heart melted. Sorry, little one—it's just not that simple! You may wish you could fire this verbally abusive woman, but unfortunately, you will have to deal with "Screaming Mimi" for the rest of your life. She's unsafe, she's totally tuned out to your needs, she's emotionally threatening and dangerous, she's a public embarrassment, but she's also yours!

What a sad world it is: Parents who love their children but don't have a clue about what went wrong between them—children who love their parents but who have been wounded too many times to trust again.

Already this family's trust bank is depleted. What horrific years are in store for them? I predict they will be bleak. We may see them on the TV talk shows ten years from now. Undoubtedly she'll be the parent who's wondering what in the world went wrong. She'll be dense, thick, unable to hear her children, or concede even an inch that admits, "I understand that that's how I make you feel. I'm sorry." I'm sure she'll still be trying to win the war instead of winning her children. She probably will be "fired"—on an emotional level at least. Her children will be the ones spewing resentment at her inability to form relationships with them.

Bring in the clouds. Watch the distance gather in families where Mom or Dad is not safe. What a sad world it is: Parents who love their children but don't have a clue about what went wrong between them—children who love their parents but who have been wounded too many times to trust again.

YOU ARE THE MEMORIES

Why is learning to be an emotionally safe parent so important? Yes, it's important for your parent-child relationship today. But, also understand that what's at stake here has wide-ranging implications beyond present-day nuclear family life. In other words, it's not just about whether all of you are getting along right now. Your children's future will not escape what's happening between you today. The quality of your parenting NOW is the grid through which the rest of your child's life will pass. It is the filter that colors and interprets their future life experiences.

You are not only making memories . . . you *are* the memories. In a deep, subconscious, inarticulated place a parent stays with his or her child . . . forever!

The adult son venting his frustration on TV with his father that day was saying that their relationship had become a scar—a wound so deep that only the grace of God will be able to stop its hemorrhaging and heal its ugliness. Far into the future, this parental wound will deepen other wounds. It is the son's primary pain that enlarges his other life difficulties.

What impact will you have on your child's future? Will your child carry a woundedness or a blessing from you? No one will love your child as a parent loves him or her. And if you don't love your child, emotionally, he or she will die.

THE SUSTAINING STRENGTH OF SOME PARENTS' LOVE

For other fortunate children, the safety of their parental relationship becomes the balm that soothes whatever difficulty life might throw their way. It is the comfort that will strengthen them throughout their lifetime. Relationship with their parents is both safe today and supporting for difficult times in the future.

I would hope to give my children the kind of sustaining love that Shari Smith's parents gave her. Her story is a testimony to the strength that loving parents can give a child to face unbelievable circumstances.

Shari was kidnapped the day before her high school graduation. Two days after her abduction, the girl's kidnapper sent her parents a two-page letter captioned "Last Will and Testament."

Without a single word of self-pity, the teenager poured out her love for her family and words of faith: "I'll be with my Father now, so please don't worry! Don't ever let this ruin your lives, and keep living one day at a time for Jesus. My thoughts will always be with you." She closed with words evoking Paul's Epistle to the Romans: "Everything works out for the good of those that love God."[1]

Shortly afterward, Shari was tortured and died at the hands of a sadistic murderer.

Where did this young girl, facing incredibly frightening circumstances, find the fortitude and presence of mind to reach out and comfort her parents at such a time?

I'm convinced that her strength was rooted in her relationship with her parents.

The strong family bond sustained Shari. Even when life had become frightening and monstrously unsafe—there was still the comfort of her parents' love.

What a precious gift they gave each other!

The quality of your parenting NOW is the grid through which the rest of your child's life will pass. It is the filter that colors and interprets their future life experiences.

You are not only making memories . . . you *are* the memories. In a deep, subconscious, inarticulated place a parent stays with his or her child . . . forever!

First Principle for Parent-Child Closeness

The following chapters will deal with eight basic relational principles that help to develop closeness with your children. All principles begin with the parent. The awesome truth is this: Parents are the key to relationship. We are responsible for establishing the relational tone. When we ask the question, "What does a child need?" an obvious answer is: A CONNECTED RELATIONSHIP WITH A PARENT WHO IS TRUSTWORTHY AND SAFE. Or let me put this another way,

RELATIONAL PRINCIPLE #1:
CHILDREN NEED PARENTS WHO ARE EMOTIONALLY SAFE.

If you care about being close to your children, then you must become an expert at communicating that you are safe. Understanding their children's perspective is extremely important to a safe parent. The relational vocabulary of the safe parent includes phrases like, "I understand why you feel that way," or "Help me to see it from your perspective." Understanding, even if you can't always agree, is the goal. When we have a hearing, when our feelings are allowed expression and validated, we can trust other people. Making the effort to understand communicates the importance of the child in his or her parent's life. Children need the safety and comfort that comes from knowing that their feelings matter to their parents. Compassionate understanding characterizes the emotionally safe parent.

What impact will you have on your child's future? Will your child carry a woundedness or a blessing from you? No one will love your child as a parent loves him or her. And if you don't love your child, emotionally, he or she will die.

A MOTIVATING LOOK INTO THE POSSIBLE FUTURE

I practice a discipline when I am feeling distant or frustrated with my children. I picture my son, somewhere in his future, struggling to provide for his family, having to work harder and harder for an unsympathetic boss until discouraged and exhausted. That possibility always motivates me to practice more tenderness today.

Picture your son in his adult years. Is he in a hospital bed, living through a personal holocaust of cancer and chemotherapy? Or could he be living with a wife who withholds love or is unfaithful to him? Is he struggling with his mental health and self-worth? Is he in some foreign prisoner-of-war camp, hungry, cold, exhausted, and longing for death? It's possible. In the future anything is possible.

If you could see an image of your daughter abused by her husband —degraded and humiliated—blackened and bruised—terrified—would you think it important to nag her about keeping her room clean today? Maybe she will have to take care of herself forever as a single woman. Is it possible that she will become a single mother in the future and prematurely age, caring alone for her children? Will her future include a car accident that leaves her disabled or disfigured? Will she struggle to survive earthquake, famine, flood, or war? Will she suffer like Shari Smith?

These are terrible thoughts. But they are also motivating thoughts. If you knew your children's future pain, wouldn't you be more nurturing today?

A parent has staying power. As a ninety-year-old woman, my grandmother, in advanced senility, would call out for her "mama" at night. Their relationship had been very close. Her mother had been dead many decades, but even in the confusion of old age, my grandmother's mother had the power to comfort and soothe her child.

The truth is—all of our children will know heartache. They all will suffer. As parents we cannot shelter them from the heartbreak of living. The question is: Will they receive from you and me the emotional resources they need to deal with the problems of life ahead? Or will dealing with their parents deplete their ability to trust and send them already wounded into their futures? Will their relationship with us be their food and sustenance for a future time? Or will we be their life-wound?

THE EMOTIONAL INGREDIENTS OF GOOD PARENTING

The next few chapters are designed to help you be a life giver, to give you a place in your children's affections by helping you to become a strong and safe place. The following chapters are the ingredients of emotionally connected parenting. They answer the question, "What does my child need from me?"

And while it's true, that we can never go back and give them just "one more hug," we have *today*. We can parent today with an eye to tomorrow. We can minimize the "if onlys." We can "lavish life" on today so that tomorrow our children will have the emotional resources to survive.

Winter is surely coming—your child will eventually experience the struggles of life (if they aren't already present)—but today is the time to be patty-caked, and hugged, and delighted in. These family years are the life holidays of kisses and laughter. These days are holy—a spiritual celebration of relationship. Winter is coming—but today is a beach, a Little League game, a prom corsage—the season that will sweeten and strengthen our children for the storms ahead.

I have always felt that laughter in the face of reality is probably the finest sound there is and will last until the day when the game is called on account of darkness. In this world, a good time to laugh is anytime you can.

LINDA ELLERBEE,
ON HER BATTLE WITH CANCER
Prime Time Live, ABC News

SIX
DANCING WITH A LIMP:
The Relatively Stable Parent

Connecting with your children involves more than simply backing away from the traditional areas of power struggle—bedtimes, clothing styles, how children spend their money, what food is eaten. Becoming a less controlling parent, by itself, would only lead you to uninvolvement, detachment, or even neglect of your children.

So when you back off from the controls, you may find that there is suddenly an enormous conversational hole. "What do we talk about now that peas and clean teeth and clothing aren't the focus of our lives?" Be aware that something else must replace the usual instructional, directional, training type of talk that passes for relational communication in many homes.

THE PROBLEM WITH FORMULAS

You can fill the gap with real talk, real relationship, and an increasing knowledge and appreciation of who your children really are.

But relationship is full of subtlety. If we fill in the conversational gap with the "right words" without real emotional honesty, we simply

71

send our children mixed messages. They will read beyond our words—to our real feelings. Say, "Sure I'd be happy to do that for you!" at the same time you are feeling enormously put upon, and your children will read the real message—*Mom or Dad resents meeting my needs*.

That's why we can't afford to "fake" the way we relate to our children, by merely saying relational words suggested by "experts."

Adjusting the words without adjusting the heart is a tempting relational shortcut—but one that can really backfire! It's like treating a bleeding wound with an aspirin. It just doesn't work! Say what your heart does not feel, and soon your children will read you as lacking in integrity, hypocritical, and unsafe. In other words, phoney.

That's why there will be no shortcut recipes to parent-child relationships in this book. There will be no formulaic approach to the things to say. No lists. No hollow words.

Instead, you need to dig deep to your inner person. There examine the things that equip you for or hinder you from the work of parenting. What do your children need from you, and what is holding you back from giving it to them? Learn what your children need from you emotionally, discipline your heart to the task, and you will be safe—a relational parent. Without this understanding, your children will learn to make a wide swath around you to avoid a relationship they regard as difficult or even dangerous.

RELATIONAL PRINCIPLE #2:
CHILDREN NEED RELATIVELY STABLE PARENTS.

Children are by nature unstable, insecure, given to anxiety. Watch how a child's world can be shattered by the seemingly smallest thing and you'll realize the long way that he or she must go to achieve stability in life. That's why children need parents who have grown past their own insecurities and achieved a degree of personal stability.

Let me be sure that you understand. I am not saying that children need *perfect, problem-free parents*. Perfect, problem-free parents would create too sterile an environment for real living. And should you be so fortunate as to go through life problem-free, your children would have no role model for problem solving. In a strange laboratory-of-life kind of way, children do need real parents complete with real problems. But, more important, children need parents who are emotionally stable in the midst of their own struggles.

SOME DANGEROUS BARRIERS
THAT HINDER CONNECTING

One of the most dangerous mistakes parents make is being unaware of their own problems . . . thinking they're stable when in reality, out of their own pain, they are hurting their children. We adults need to take a long, hard look at our own emotional health. Are there signs of irrational anger, depression, anxiety, or patterns of relational problems? Do these areas have an impact on our relationship to our kids? Are we wounding our children with the snags and jagged edges of our own lives?

It's hard for a child to trust an adult who is like an emotional yo-yo—loving one minute, angry and explosive the next. An unpredictable parent, one given to wide emotional swings, is an unstable parent. Rage-aholics, verbally abusive parents, screamers, yellers, undo all the positive they try to build into their relationships with their children. No birthday present, special gift, or family outing can convince a child that such a parent is emotionally safe.

It's also hard to connect with a parent who is depressed and distant. How does a child reach a parent whose own emotional needs drive him or her to alcoholism or workaholism?

How do you connect with a parent who is empty inside—an emotionally hollow breather of air? How can you trust such a parent to meet your needs when his or her own neediness is always taking the center stage of family life? Most children learn to give up relationally on such a self-preoccupied parent.

Becoming a parent should motivate moms and dads to care for themselves emotionally. Sometimes we meet our children's needs by meeting our own needs. It seems like a paradox, but it's true. *Take care of your emotional health for the sake of your child.* If you love your child, you should be willing to do any preventive work that keeps you from passing on your own problems to your child. And along the way, you will be doing yourself an enormous favor as well.

Becoming emotionally stable—emotionally safe—may be the hardest interior work you will ever have to do.

This is not a simple project. It's not a matter of simply becoming the parental Pied Piper of your children's world by pasting on a phoney smile and piping a major tune through the house, hoping to "fix" your home.

It means doing the hard, interior work of becoming emotionally well yourself.

Becoming emotionally stable—emotionally safe—may be the hardest interior work you will ever have to do.

MY OLD NEMESIS—DEPRESSION

I know. It was my biggest parental challenge.

Not long ago I was interviewed for a radio program about parenting. The interviewer threw me a hard question. She asked me, "What are you most proud about in your parenting?"

To be "proud" about something implies that I had a struggle or made an enormous effort to overcome a problem area. It was a nice way of asking me what I struggled with as a parent. My mind easily located what had been my biggest parental challenge—but had I met that difficulty with enough success to feel "proud"?

I plunged in, "My biggest struggle as a parent has been being emotionally stable. My children were born to me during the saddest period of my life."

I went on to explain that my personal life had taken an overwhelmingly depressive turn—right in the midst of my pregnancy and early parental years.

"Daddy's sick!" the voice at the other end of the phone had said.

I would learn that "Daddy's sick!" was an enormous understatement. My father had contracted encephalitis, and his brain was burned beyond function. Daddy would never recognize any of us again. He would never again say our names or any other word. He had no memory or ability to learn. He literally had no ideas! Daddy, as we had known him, was gone. Our family was devastated.

I was three months pregnant with Brendan, and Daddy's condition would be the dark cloud that would hang over my birthing and early mothering for the next four and a half years until his death. For four and a half years I worked hard to hold back tears about him every day. For four and a half years the thought or sight of him broke my heart. For four and a half years I would wake with a leaden heart, knowing that the reality of that day would be unlike the beautiful dreams that had restored my father to me during the night.

There I was—a young mom—juggling birth and impending death, wondering if it was time to laugh or time to break down and cry. I was grieving for my dad—how could I be happy with my babies?

I was on precarious emotional ground as far as raising my own children was concerned. I knew it. I worried about the emotional cues they were learning from me—the distant, sad look—the flat emotions—the lack of emotional energy for positive things since it was all being used to simply function and mourn. What would my children remember about me? Their sad mom? Was that the legacy I was doomed to leave them—a heritage of tears and sighing?

COLLIDING SEASONS!

Life is so intense! In the renowned passage from Ecclesiastes 3, we're given a taste of the wide spectrum of emotional experiences of a lifespan. We're told that "there is a time for everything and a season for every activity under heaven":

> *a time to be born and a time to die,*
> *a time to plant and a time to uproot,*
> *a time to kill and a time to heal,*
> *a time to tear down and a time to build,*
> *a time to weep and a time to laugh,*
> *a time to mourn and a time to dance. . . .*

This Scripture affirms the wide range of our emotional response to life situations. We are created as emotional beings capable of a spectrum of deep feelings. Our emotions, positive and negative, are a natural response to life. Our emotions are valid.

But I have found that real life seldom behaves with the poetic organization of Ecclesiastes 3. A time to weep collides with a time to laugh. A time to be born refuses to be compartmentalized and squeezes into the time-to-die season. We plant with one hand while the other is uprooting. Our tears inhabit our laughter. In real life we find ourselves dancing on graves and mourning at births. Life can be so messy!

If we aren't careful, the sadder experiences easily overwhelm our ability to appreciate and enjoy our own children.

Yes, we're thrilled about becoming parents—the baby comes, and he or she brings such happiness. But here's the catch—with all that baby magic they still don't possess the power to clear the way of tragedies.

> Without a conscious parental effort to be emotionally whole, to turn from the sad and ugly and unfair, and reposition toward the pure and lovely and right, we will teach our children negatively from the core of our own struggling emotional life.

Babies are born, and at the same time there's a death of a friend or family member.

Babies come, and some "dads" or "moms" decide to leave and abandon the responsibility of family.

Babies arrive right in the middle of divorce or disease or job loss.

Babies make you a parent while you are still struggling with unresolved relational issues with your own parents. Have you noticed that life provides a constant flow of reasons to be sad or angry or bitter or afraid? Babies and children live right in the middle of parental stress.

Without a conscious parental effort to be emotionally whole, to turn from the sad and ugly and unfair, and reposition toward the pure and lovely and right, we will teach our children negatively from the core of our own struggling emotional life.

EARLY RELATIONSHIP MATTERS

Sinichi Suzuki, world-renowned music educator, wrote about the importance of early environment on children, drawing from nature:

> The first month in a nightingale's life determines its fate. I had always thought that a nightingale's incomparable song was instinctive and inherited. But it is not so.
> Nightingales to be used as pets are taken as fledglings from nests of wild birds in the spring. As soon as they lose their fear and accept food, a "master bird" is borrowed that daily sings its lovely song, and the infant bird listens for a period of about a month. In this way the little wild bird is trained by the master bird.
> If it has a good teacher, the infant bird will learn from experience to produce as beautiful tones as its teacher. But if an infant bird is brought to such a teacher after being raised by wild nightingales, there is always failure, as long experience has shown.[1]

The illustration of the nightingales reminds me that many children's problems could be solved if they just had parents who were "good singers"—moms and dads who understand the importance of early emotional environment on children—parents who take responsibility for the mood or emotional tone of the home—parents who understand that their children are absorbing the emotional atmosphere and learning to respond to life as their moms and dads did. (I am very sensitive to the tone of voice that is used in our home. We have carried this to the point of investing in a house intercom so that we aren't screaming at one another between floors. Yelling at or for each other, even if it's not in anger, sets a strident atmosphere. It's too short a step to using that voice in anger with each other, which, I believe is inappropriate and abusive. We believe it's been a good relational investment!)

IF MAMA AIN'T HAPPY, AIN'T NOBODY HAPPY!

There is more truth to that T-shirt's saying, "If Mama ain't happy, ain't nobody happy!" than many of us realize. Like nightingales—children pick up clues about the emotional side of life from the environment of their parents.

> Children learn from their parents whether life is a wonderful adventure or an endurance of one disappointment after another.

Some fortunate children will be blessed with parents who are aware of the effect of the emotional environment on their children and are careful about the lessons they teach. These children will draw from their parents' emotional cues positive conclusions about themselves and life itself.

But other children will be exposed to "wild" undisciplined parents—parents who set a critical tone, angry atmosphere, or use loud, abusive voices, parents bowed down by their own problems and life difficulties, and these children's experiences will be less successful, even damaging, because of the negative emotional environment to which their parents have exposed them.

Children learn from their parents whether life is a wonderful adventure or an endurance of one disappointment after another. They draw life perceptions from the core of their parent's emotional life. Thus, children of depressed parents learn depressive-thinking patterns. Children of angry parents learn to yell and strike out at others.

ALWAYS DANCING SEASON

That's why, when it comes to parenting children—it needs to be a time to dance—regardless of what else is happening. No matter what is occurring in your life, your child needs you to be as emotionally whole and positive as possible.

It's a matter of focus. Job describes this parental dilemma (Job 14). Notice where the troubled parent spends his or her emotional energy: "If his sons are honored, he does not know it. If they are brought low, he does not see it. He feels but the pain of his own body and mourns only for himself."

You see, a troubled parent is a self-centered parent. A troubled parent lives life at a survival level. Period.

That's why it's important to take a hard look at our own emotional health. We can't be a need-meeter for our children if we are consumed with our own problems.

Have you made peace with your own parents? Have you embraced your past—the good along with the bad? Have you done the hard emotional work of growing whole? Do you understand forgiveness? We all have our share of bumps and bruises, but the parent who has not dealt with his or her own pain wields a dangerous emotional stick.

"Hurt people hurt people,"[2] says Dr. Sandra Wilson. She is absolutely right!

It's true that even abusive parents have loving feelings toward their children, but their unresolved pain eventually makes their children the focus of their emotional flashpoints.

GET HELP!

For years, I've watched a friend of mine battle PMS. What a struggle! She claims that all of her children have been affected by living with a mother who regularly, monthly, turns their home into an emotional war zone. She once confided in me, with a great deal of remorse, that she lost her oldest child because her childhood came and went before my friend was able to receive help for her problem. She sacrificed this daughter to emotional outbursts over insignificant things. Another child has learned to communicate through emotional outbursts and exacerbated sighs, behavior that looks suspiciously like her mother's; another child is an expert at avoidance—making wide swaths around her.

When I asked what she would advise for other women, she sympathetically counseled, "Tell them that nothing is worth becoming so upset over that you alienate your family. If you suffer—your family suffers. Get help!"

Emotionally safe parents are emotionally stable parents, free to focus on the needs of their children. If you are struggling to focus on your children's needs because of your own pain—get help! Don't wait until your children have passed through their childhoods!

We have so little control of what comes into our lives—no choice over the things we must learn to deal with. And have you noticed that life can really pour it on? Almost daily, I still have to make a conscious effort to choose to focus on what's positive, not on what's negative. Sometimes I'm not sure I've been successful in teaching joyful songs to my children, because I'm aware of the inner struggle going on all the time.

Did I have something to be "proud" of about my parenting? Had I beat depression?

As a young mother, I knew what I wanted. I wanted a home where there was laughter. I wanted the courage to live life joyfully, although it could be full of heartache and disillusionment sometimes. I wanted to celebrate life and drink deeply from the wells of gladness. I knew on some emotional level that I was "lame"—wounded by Dad's tragedy and walking with an emotional limp—but I wanted to learn how to leap for joy. That's what I wanted for my children.

So I set out to establish a positive, healthy emotional tone for my home. My plan was a simple one: I would take responsibility for that emotional tone. It would begin with me. I would greet my babies with joy, whether it was the middle of the night to breastfeed or to calm a bad dream. I would let my children know that they gave me pleasure. The childhood bogeymen who dwell in dark places, the fear of the things that go bump in the night, my own grief for my father would be chased away with reassuring joy. I would never just go through the motions zombie-like in the middle of some sleep-robbed night, but I would connect emotionally and lift the fear and gloom with reassuring happiness. That is what I tried to do.

When my children took the emotional low road (a tendency in most children), I disciplined myself to take the high road. When children are left to their own emotional resources, they will often set the tone at the lowest rung:

"No one likes me!"

"I never get picked for a team."

"I'm bored. This is a terrible day!"

"I hate (fill in the blank) . . ."

Ever heard these kinds of things from your kids? Negative! Negative! Negative!

I refused to live on that level. I became adult. When they whined, I refused to whine back . . . I smiled and reassured them they would survive! When they were angry, I tried not to let the situation become catastrophic by getting angry myself. I said by my attitude in a million different ways, "Life isn't so bad—you can trust me to help you remember that when your immaturity and lack of life experience threatens to blow you away emotionally, I will not be blown away."

While I taught my children, I was reinforcing the life lessons I myself needed to learn. And so, even while my heart wore mourning for my father, I learned to delight in the things I could.

Yes, my father was dying a slow, shattering death—that was our everyday agony. But, my children had ten perfect fingers and ten toes ripe for tickling. Yes, my father would never say my name again, but, to Brendan and Justin I was "Mommy." I had a new name, a name I loved. Yes, my father was dwelling in an unreachable part of his soul, but Brendan and Justin were bright, eager learners, open to everything to which they were exposed.

When there are children in our life—it's always dancing season—even if we must occasionally dance with a limp!

Life is intense. But it can be as intensely joyful as it is sorrowful. I choose to mix my life's cup with acceptance of its pain and celebration of its joys. What a brew! I am determined not to let sadness overcome joy. I am a blessed woman, and I will experience that reality every time I choose to cuddle, tickle, laugh with, or enjoy my children.

Sometimes we parents cry. We don't need to deny the reality of grief or sadness. We don't need to hide that part of life from our children. But neither should we feel guilt at experiencing the positive side of the emotional spectrum. When there are children in our life—it's always dancing season—even if we must occasionally dance with a limp!

A SON'S BLESSING

That was the journey I started over eighteen years ago. I guess that's why I cherish a note my oldest son, Brendan, wrote me recently.

My heart stopped for a moment.

Mom,

Do you know what I'm going to remember most about you? I'll always remember how sparky and cheerful you are—and how much you seem to enjoy life. You make me feel happy and cheerful. You're fun to be around.

Brendan

What words for a person struggling with depressive tendencies to hear! Oh, the comfort of those words that Brendan casually blessed me with that day! He had no idea! From the mouth of one of my babes I'd learned that I'd won the battle against my old adversary—depression. He'd seen my tears, but he remembered my laughter. He knew my heartbreak, but he remembered my joy. The discipline of greeting the nighttime parenting chores with joy, of laughing even with a dull ache in my heart, of celebrating life in the shadow of death, had been fruitful. Oh, thank you, Brendan! I'm not sure I deserved his appraisal—but I guess you could say that it made me, well, "proud"!

I also know something that even my son may not have realized about his mother. I know there are still days when I walk with an emotional limp. Honestly, life has never seemed as secure, my sense of wellbeing so intact since my father's illness and death. Life seems painfully fragile and precarious at times, but I have chosen to set my fear to the most joyful music. I accept the sad and the joyful as a part of my life. They dwell together on most days. But I am hoping that to my children it is not so much a limp as a dance. I am becoming whole, although I am not perfectly there. And that's all right. If you walked with me for a while, you might mistake my halt for a jig—which it certainly is.

DANCE WITH A LIMP, IF YOU MUST—BUT DANCE!

I hope it will be your conscious choice to dance and sing during your child-raising years—regardless of your pain and struggle—for on an emotional and spiritual level, you are giving your children dancing and singing lessons.

These years of living with you will be the emotional heritage they will draw on to deal with their own life journey. It's important when they experience difficulties that they know that EVERYONE—even their own parents—struggles in life. But, it is to be hoped, they are learning that they need not be blown away by their problems, either.

What kind of emotional tone are you setting in your home? Are you emotionally positive? Are you honest about your pain but committed not to let that overwhelm your joy? Do the emotional cues you give your child about life reassure him or her that living is a valuable experience and worth the bother? Are you attractive emotionally—a positive teacher? Are you stable enough to be emotionally safe? Are you emotionally available and easy to connect with? Are you a secure, strong, presence in your child's life?

WHEN I WAS A KID, THE RUSSIANS WERE ALWAYS COMING!

While I was growing up in the '50s, my family attended a church where a favorite theme of the preacher was, "The Russians are coming!" His apocalyptic messages filled me with fear.

I bought it completely!

I remember lying in my bed after a Sunday-night service, feeling full of anxiety about the future. I would never get married or have children. We would all be blown to smithereens!

Downstairs I could hear my parents with their friends—all "aunts" and "uncles" to us children, in the Baptist tradition. Their laughter would drift upstairs.

Dad would sit down at the piano and play gospel music to which you could almost dance. They would sing. Oh, the crazy, intoxicating ring of their laughter! The strength of their voices! How they loved life! My fears didn't have a chance when Mom and Dad were laughing!

Maybe the Russians were coming—like the preacher had warned—but for tonight, Mom and Dad were celebrating! It felt as though all was right with *my* little world, at least.

Maybe we should stop and build a bomb shelter—but how could we when Mom and Dad were so busy dancing?

Maybe we would all be reduced to ashes in a great mushroom cloud, but today we were singing!

Laughing! Dancing! Singing!

And how the memory of their laughing, dancing, and singing strengthens and comforts me even today!

During these family years—while your children are getting their emotional cues from you—learn to sing. If you love your babes, kick up your heels and learn to sing well! Let your laughter teach your children that all is well, that life is worth living, and worth living to the full.

If you are a person of faith—and I make a distinction between those who are simply religious and those who trust God—then you have an enormous advantage in the area of emotional health and stability.

AN UNSHAKABLE FOUNDATION

The wisdom of the biblical literature says, "Those who trust in the Lord are steady as Mount Zion, unmoved by any circumstance" (Psalm 125:1 TLB).

"He who fears the Lord has a secure fortress, and for his children it will be a refuge" (Proverbs 14:26) .

There *is* a time for everything and a season for every activity under heaven. For those of us raising children, this is the season of family living. *Strengthen your heart.* Work on your own jagged edges. Be a stable force and strong tower—steady as mount Zion. Learn to sing! Learn to laugh! Pick up those feet and dance—with a limp if you must—but *dance!*

Being a stable person is the second principle toward becoming the "warm, loving," relational parent your children need.

And while you boogie and sashay, tap and jitterbug, two-step and fox-trot, you will not be dancing alone—you will be dancing right into your child's heart.

For God has given us these times of joy. . . .

PSALM 81:4 (TLB)

SEVEN
HUCKLEBERRY DAYS:
The Fun Parent

When it comes to getting into your child's heart, a good question to ask is, "Am I fun to live with?" Scientists tells us that animal infants tend to bond to the first thing they see moving. Undoubtedly, sometime in the future, after millions of research dollars have been spent, scientists will inform us of something we already suspect: Human infants bond to the first thing they see laughing!

No doubt about it—children are attracted to joy and laughter and fun. They have a natural affinity for people who are upbeat. It makes sense. Think about it, if these pairs entered a room, to whom would you gravitate?

Eeyore or Tigger?

Mr. Wilson or Mr. Rogers?

Lucy or Snoopy?

Miss Piggy or Kermit?

We all learn to avoid the person who's a walking cloud on legs, the person who darkens the room when he or she enters. The man or woman who sags, sighs, dumps, and negatively emotes is the person we naturally sidestep.

We are attracted to positive emotional energy—which leads us to the third relational principle.

RELATIONAL PRINCIPLE #3:
CHILDREN NEED PARENTS WHO ARE FUN!

But, is this really a need? Or just something that all kids would like to have?

Remember, we're talking about building connected relationships—not just providing the things a child needs to survive. We want to build into our parental repertoire the things that are attractive to children, the things that help them to connect and feel attached to us. The fun parent differs somewhat from the stable parent. The craziness of the fun parent is the frosting on the cake of the stable parent. Or you could think of the fun parent as being the stable parent but revved up a few notches.

Kids love this!

THE ATTRACTION DYNAMIC

I first observed this attraction dynamic when I was a student teacher. My instructor was a classroom music teacher—Miss Fritsch. She was not much taller than the grade-school children she was teaching—and at least four times wider than they were. She wasn't the type you'd typically think children would be attracted to, but when she walked into the classroom, it was MAGIC!

Her off-the-wall humor punctuated her music classes. This was no long-haired stuffy musician! The children never knew what to expect from her—except that it was going to be fun! As a student teacher in the inner city, I noted that Miss Fritsch had no "discipline problems" in her classes. I never saw her reprimand a child. It was obvious that the children adored her!

"Valerie, there is something to praise in every child. Even if you can only say, 'Hey, those are great shoes you've got on there!'" This was her daily admonishment to me. Seemingly without effort, she focused on what was positive and praiseworthy in every child. That, mixed with an enormous dose of zany humor, was her philosophy of teaching.

It worked! The children loved her! They learned!

Her way of celebrating Halloween was especially absurd. The week before, she would poll the children on what they would like her to wear to their classroom. She teased that she was also a trick-or-treater. The children didn't believe her. She told them her Halloween wardrobe included a pink tutu, a football uniform, or baby clothes, complete with diaper, undershirt, pacifier, and teddy bear.

With few exceptions, the ballerina costume was the hands-down winner in most classrooms. On Halloween, to their amazement and delight, she would show up at class in her pink tulle ballet costume and toe shoes. She didn't just walk into the classroom—she made a grand entrance! With the record player blasting "Swan Lake," she performed arabesques, turns on point, pliés, a pas de deux with an imaginary partner. Folds of pale goose-bumpy middle-aged skin rolled in great waves out of armholes. Doughy knees punctuated blue-veined varicose thighs and calves. Over-permed hair frizzed over a lopsided rhinestone tiara. Topping it all off was a wicked smile.

She was a sight! And she knew it!

She was the first one to laugh at herself!

How could you help but love this enchantingly eccentric woman? She cast her spell on me as well as the students in her classes. Contrary to the traditional advice given to new teachers, "Don't smile until after Thanksgiving," Miss Fritsch immediately went for the funny bone. She knew that humor was the way to her students' hearts.

WE PARENTS TAKE OURSELVES TOO SERIOUSLY

So, what does Miss Fritsch have to do with parenting? Well, I believe that most parents, including myself, could stand to have a little of Miss Fritsch rub off on them. It seems to me, that as a general rule, we take ourselves much too seriously. The ability to laugh at ourselves can be the basis for much family fun and emotional bonding.

Are you often totally crazy and off-the-wall with your children? Is mealtime fun or just a functional drag? Can you tell a decent joke? (A great art, you know!) Can you see what's charming and funny in your kids? Or have you allowed the pace and stress of modern living to squeeze fun from your relationship with your children?

The ability to laugh at ourselves can be the basis for much family fun and emotional bonding.

Shared laughter is like family glue. It is the stuff of family well-being and all-is-well thoughts. It brings us together as few other things can.

Parents who are interested in developing their children's musical talents give them music lessons, take them to concerts, and play music in the home. Parents who are interested in developing their children's athletic abilities sign them up for soccer and T-ball, take them to games, and play catch in the backyard. It follows that parents who are interested in developing their child's ability to delight in life should fill their home with laughter. Happy children catch that joy from parents who enjoy life. Shared laughter is like family glue. It is the stuff of family well-being and all-is-well thoughts. It brings us together as few other things can.

WHAT JOY LOOKS LIKE AT HOME

Joy is an indicator of family health. What does this look like in family life?

1. Self-satisfaction—the sense of secure, comfortable membership in the community—is almost ever-present. This includes the family community as well as various segments of social structure—neighborhood, city, country. (The family does not operate in isolation. The family has "people over." The family entertains. The family welcomes their children's invitations to friends. Home is a warm, entertaining place.)

2. The family likes to be together—especially from early on in the lives of their children—trips to the zoo, picnics, extended-family affairs, weddings, parties, and so forth.

3. The family especially enjoys celebration of joyous events—family births, weddings, confirmations, birthdays, graduations, achievements, completion of projects, and so forth.

4. The family enjoys the commonplace—eating together, talking, walking, going to a movie, working in or on the house together, visiting, and all the activities that comprise the everyday stuff of life.

5. The family laughs out loud *often*. They are able to "let go" with welcome abandon.[1]

Think of the times when you laughed so hard you cried. Remember the sense of inner massage and well-being that kind of experience gave you?

Absurdly, Embarrassingly Fun to Be With

My husband, Steve, has a loud, out-of-control laugh. Laughter comes easily to him. Even from his sleep he often wakes with a deep belly laugh from one of his dreams. Our youngest son says, "Dad doesn't have nightmares, he has laughmares!" It's almost as if he's retained the abandoned laughter that's so charming in children. It would be embarrassing to sit with him in public places if his laugh weren't so infectious. It's also embarrassing that his sense of humor can be pathetically unsophisticated. For instance, we had to hold him in his seat when we took him to see *Beethoven*—a kids' movie with a deep redemptive plot—about a dog who makes a lot of doggie doo-doo messes in the house.

Most adults endured the movie, but not Steve. The boys and I stopped watching the movie about half way through—watching Dad was so much more entertaining! Tears ran down his crimson face, his veins popped out—adding to his complete facial distortion. He held his stomach and bent forward and sideways. He would have been on the floor if we weren't holding on to him. He was raucous! Worst of all, he didn't appear to notice or care that he was the only one "losing it" in the theater. Everyone stared.

The boys and I exchanged eye-rolling, he's-doing-it-again glances. We slouched down in our seats, trying to be invisible. We moved away from him a few seats, hoping that people would think we weren't with him. But we laughed. We laughed at Dad. We were a row of public idiots! Tears streamed down our embarrassed faces!

He was a sight! He was out of control! He was (we hated to admit it) charming! He was absurdly, embarrassingly fun to be with!

But even in our family, it seems that the spaces between such experiences can be too wide. Great, classic masterpiece movies like *Beethoven* are just too few and far between! Sometimes, parents have to initiate family fun. Here are some ideas we've tried.

Ideas for Family Fun Your Kids Will Love

- Why not get your kids up in the middle of the night to go to the all-night discount store? It could be so much fun to see who shows up in their hair-rollers and pajamas! Get to know your local insomniacs! Better yet, meet a few other families at the blue-light special and follow it up with an early-morning breakfast at some all-night restaurant.

- Throw a tacky party. Send invitations on used greeting cards—scribble the details on the sides, or cross out the previous information. Make sure everyone dresses really tastelessly. One of our friends wore a green plaid leisure suit, a cowboy hat, and a political button that said, "Elect Richard Nixon." As they drove through town to our party, he stuck his head out the window and yelled, "I am Jennifer's father!" A really tacky thing to do to a thirteen-year-old girl!

  Serve junk food—anything wrapped in cellophane will do—Ho Ho's, Twinkies, marshmallow snowballs, Fritos, beef jerky, enormous kosher pickles, and Jolt (double the caffeine soda). Decorate with crepe-paper streamers.

  Say tacky things like, "Are you pregnant *again*?" or "Did you know you have bad breath?" Cover your furniture with plastic. Tell boring stories, with all the unimportant details. Play polka music. Insist that everyone dances. Show slides of your family vacation. Rent a port-a-potty and lock the bathroom doors. For the front lawn, rent a flashing sign that proclaims, TACKY PARTY IN PROGRESS!

You get the picture.

- Create a "Better Home Than Garden Award" for a friend's yard. With your children in tow, sneak (under cover of darkness) into a good friend's yard and plant pink plastic flamingos in a prominent spot. Include a poem around the flamingo's neck that informs your friends that should the flamingos be removed before a two-week period, other more obnoxious lawn ornaments will appear—yard ornaments that glow in the dark and have moving parts. This award can be passed from deserving yard to deserving yard, with everyone's children getting in on the fun.
- Have a "You must have been a beautiful baby!" party. This is particularly good when your children are entering puberty and are already excruciatingly self-conscious. Invite your friends to bring their slides and family movies for a fun night

of *ooh*ing and *ah*ing at all the darling old pictures. Moms and dads should bring their baby pictures, too!

- Pack your kids' suitcases and show up after school some Friday. Take them on a surprise adventure—to the city for a day, camping by a lake, to the theater or major-league baseball game, to some friend's house for the weekend.

- Invest in some comedy tapes. You might try some Abbott and Costello radio tapes, or any other type of humor your family enjoys. Instead of music as you travel, listen to comedy and enjoy laughing together. So many books are available on tape these days, including kiddies' lit, which is full of humorous irony. Our family has gathered through the years a collection that we loan to other traveling families. We find it really helps the travel time to pass in an enjoyable way.

- Occasionally do something that blows your children's minds. I have always been opposed to street motorcycles, so it amazed my children (and shocked their dad) when I went out, without their father, and purchased two used dirt-bike motorcycles. They haven't quite gotten over it. They still point out to people that *Mom* was the one who bought the motorcycles.

In this same category, I remember one particular Fourth of July. The boys had bought an arsenal of fireworks—something illegal in our home state but not in the state we were visiting. We found a secluded place and had our own fireworks display. My job was to keep the car's headlights on our family of pyromaniacs until the fuses were lit. When Steve yelled, "Run!" I would turn off the headlights. In the dark, the kids would scatter, enjoying the danger. Until 1:00 A.M., again and again the scene was repeated, with children and father becoming more adventurous and excited.

There were no houses in sight, we probably weren't bothering anyone, but the whole escapade had the feel of contributing to the delinquency of a minor. I was apprehensive. Picturing Steve and me ending up in one of those legendary small-town jails, I kept waiting for the police—or worse, a farmer with a shotgun—to come. I could imagine that our children would be taken from us by the child-protection agency, that our pictures would be plastered in newspapers across America with the headline: "More Christian Broadcasters in Jail!"

Gosh, it was fun!

- Try a Huckleberry Day. This is based on the children's book called Freaky Friday, where the parents and children exchange roles for a day. In our family, a Huckleberry Day is where the family gets in the car, but the children decide where the car goes, how the designated money is spent, if and when the family has lunch. We call it a Huckleberry Day because it's like getting on Huckleberry Finn's raft and just adventuring with the flow of the stream.

Originally, I thought this would be a harmless way to give a child a sense of power for a day. I didn't realize how much I would learn about my children's likes and dislikes, or what adventures we would have when my children were calling the shots. On Huckleberry Days we've visited baseball-card shops, eaten ice-cream cones for lunch, and explored towns we've never visited before.

Things tend to happen on Huckleberry Days that are funny in retrospect. There was the time when my youngest son, Justin, and I were wandering through the mountains of western North Carolina and had a flat tire in the middle of nowhere—at least the view was breathtaking!

MARY POPPINS DOES STATESVILLE

Or the time when Justin was nine, and he and I ended up in Joliet, Illinois. We were lost. As I was driving and trying to read the map, I ran over an enormous piece of cardboard that wedged itself between the frame and the tires of the van. We had to stop. Very slowly, with the underside of the van screeching and rubbing against the cardboard, we limped into the first gas station we saw.

It just happened to be right across the street from the maximum-security prison.

Cautiously, I got out of our van. A crowd had gathered at this gas station, and they were not happy. It seems they had come to visit the prison inmates, but the prison had been put into lockdown because a guard had been killed. They were shaking their arms at the walls of the prison. They were screaming from huddled groupings in what seemed like a million different languages.

I was wearing a white sailor Laura Ashley summer dress and was uncomfortably aware of looking like Mary Poppins in this particular crowd. They looked at me as if I were going to break into a verse of "Just a Spoonful of Sugar Helps the Medicine Go Down!" I was decidedly out of place.

"Stay in the car!" I warned Justin. I watched his eyes widen as I approached the most harmless looking man I could find.

"Could you help me? I need to get this cardboard unwedged from my car."

He barely looked at me but mumbled something I couldn't understand.

"Pardon? I didn't understand what you said."

"Mmmverow bvoiwpmvios!" he said.

"Excuse me—I'm having some trouble here."

Once more he said something like, "Moinsemngos!" I obviously didn't get it! Shrugging his shoulders with an "I give up!" motion, realizing there was probably no other way to get rid of this ditzy woman foolish enough to dress like an escapee from a Disney movie in this crowd, he crawled under my car and dislodged the cardboard.

"Oh, thank you! I really do appreciate your help!" I gushed as I got closer to him. "Could I pay you for your trouble?"

"NLLIYLMNKJY!" he responded, shaking his head in disgust. And then I saw it. The poor man had no tongue! The terrible possibilities of how he had lost his tongue flashed through my imagination. Street fights! Torture! A terrible accident or disfiguring operation! How terrible for him! How embarrassing for me! I hadn't understood what he had been trying to say to me. He had probably been trying to tell me to shove off, but I just hadn't got the message!

Oh, boy! This could have been really ugly.

With an enormous sigh, I climbed into the driver's seat, locked the doors, and drove away, still lost. As we left that angry scene, Justin suggested in a shaky little voice that on our next Huckleberry Day we ought to bring Dad along.

It helps to have a little street-savvy if you are going to be an adventurer!

There have been enough of these *Perils of Pauline* instances on Huckleberry Days that you can understand why my son says, "Mom, you're a little bit of a ditz!" He's not really being disrespectful. He's just expressing the truth about my less-than-together side. He always says it with a smile and something like affection in his eyes. I take it in the spirit in which it's given. When you're a very human parent, it helps to be the first one to laugh at your own idiot side! Why not? My theory is the rest of the family is laughing, I might as well join in!

- Have a picnic at midnight.
- Rent rollerblades and take off work for the day to join in a "family skate."
- Stay up all night for a family film festival, with each family member picking his or her favorite video.
- Show your family slides or movies on the side of your house one night—kind of like a family drive-in, for the whole neighborhood to see.

The possibilities are limitless!

THE KEY POINT. DON'T MISS THIS!

But maybe as you read the above suggestions, you're thinking, "That doesn't sound like fun to me!" Well, that's possible, and it doesn't necessarily mean that your sense of humor is stunted. But you may have missed a key point about becoming attractive and fun to your children: *Family fun should be kid-friendly.* To be the stuff of family bonding, it should be the kind of fun that kids enjoy.

Be playful! That's the kind of fun that becomes the stuff of family history.

YOU'RE NOT FUNNY? THEN MAKE FRIENDS WHO ARE

What about parents who just aren't the crazy kind? What if you tend to be more serious and intense? I have a great suggestion for you: Make friends with funny people!

As I look back on our family years, I realize this has been a contributing factor in our fun times together. Much of our fun was experienced in community. It's true. Steve and I have been members of a life-support group for nearly ten years. For ten years we've been praying and laughing and loving the same five couples and their children. I have concluded that Steve and I are much more fun in combination with others. Through the years, these wonderful friends have stretched our capacity for fun to a memorable degree. Early on, we made a commitment to regularly include our children in our activities. In retrospect, it was a decision that's proven to be exceptionally wise. Our children have been laughed at, photographed, videoed, prayed over, and loved by many other families in our group during their childhood years. I'm sure that the shared laughter will be one of their cherished childhood memories.

I guess that's a wonderful advantage to sharing your life within the context of the church. The fun tends to grow and include children whose parents may not be all that spontaneous and full of life.

Recently we talked about disbanding our group. We all agree that our lives are becoming more complicated as our children age. It's harder to make all the meetings. Several of us travel regularly. But the children had an interesting reaction—particularly the younger children. They were alarmed! They didn't want the fun to stop before they are grown! I think they are right. They would really miss something if we all stopped celebrating life together!

Think about the adults you loved as a child. What drew you to them? My grandmother loved a practical joke. She loved to shorten an unsuspecting sheet. Christmas presents for the men in her life were home-made boxer shorts embroidered with hearts or flowers. The wrappings of her gifts were always elaborate and flowery, leading the receiver to think they were receiving a serious present. I still remember her delighted snicker when the embarrassed male held up his present for the entire family to see.

When you go with laughter, when you're fun, you will never travel alone.
Your children will travel with you.

In my father's family there was an odd tradition of telling funny stories about the family member who had just passed away. It was a way of publicly recognizing the funny but endearing qualities of someone they loved. The laughter helped break the tension and ease the pain. It acknowledged that we love people because they make us laugh, because they give us pleasure in so many individualistic, quirky but endearing ways.

The generation of family members with names like Bertha, Millard, Dewey, Cordelia, and Will were all laid to rest with loving laughter from my dad's family.

It's not a bad way to go.

Nor is it a bad way to travel through life. When you go with laughter, when you're fun, you will never travel alone.

Your children will travel with you.

Children need more than food, shelter and clothing. The bottom line is: Every child needs at least one person who's crazy about him.

FRAN STOTT
*Dean, Erickson Institute
for Advanced Study in Child Development*

EIGHT
"EVERYBODY'S WEIRD IN THEIR OWN SPECIAL WAY"*
The Loyal Parent

It had been a particularly long night of mothering for Christine. Jonathan, her three-year-old, had been sick with stomach flu. She had spent the night helping him make trips to the bathroom—and then after rubbing his back and comforting him back to sleep, she had to clean floors, sheets, and blankets. What a night!

Wearily she had managed to sleep a couple of hours just as the sun was beginning to dawn. But it was the sleep of mothers—light, with one ear open, waiting for the alarm that signaled another run for the bathroom.

She heard it in her sleep. The turning of her bedroom doorknob, the dragging of jammied feet on the bare wood floors. Before she was even conscious, she was thinking, *"Oh, no! He's back!"*

She opened her eyes, and there was Jonathan standing beside her bed. He carried his blanket, and his eyes looked amazingly bright, all

*Title of paper written by Justin Bell in his fourth grade Creative Writing class.

things considered. Then, smiling at her, he announced, "Here I am, Mom! Your bundle of joy!"

Here I am, Mom! Your bundle of joy! Wouldn't it be wonderful if our children had that kind of confidence about how we feel about them—even in the worst moments?

Unfortunately, many children never experience that type of unconditional acceptance, security, and belonging that comes from knowing you are the delight of your parents' life.

ENJOYING OUR CHILDREN LESS

Maybe that's because some of us parents are becoming—well, a little weird. We tend these days to enjoy our children less. Many parents are just working too hard at making their children into trophies of their parenting skills. Enmeshment abounds!

This is how one writer described our tendencies, "We sidle up to the neighbor's refrigerator magnet montage and surreptitiously scan her kid's report card.

We psychoanalyze every playground encounter.

We not only study our kids, we study their homework.

We're into overparenting.

Everyone knows someone who's gone off the common-sense cliff. Our parental theme song is Sting's anthem to obsession: 'Every breath you take, every move you make, I'll be watching you.'"[2]

PARENTS WHO WANT THEIR CHILDREN TO MAKE THEM LOOK GOOD

Perhaps one of the most dangerous aspects of the interfering parental style is the tendency to become overinvolved in our children's achievements or lack thereof. Interfering parents can view their children primarily as extensions of themselves. Because what other people think matters so much to them, to a distorted degree, interfering parents believe their children reflect back on them. With this mindset, it then becomes extremely important for the child to make the parent look good. An enormous amount of energy goes into the pursuit of family image-making. Sadly, this approach also robs the family of the energy needed to develop real relationships based on trust and unconditional love. This is a shameful misuse of children. It is a deep disloyalty to the intrinsic child. Unfortunately, it is the deal that is currently being struck between many a parent and child.

Everyone knows parents who become overinvolved with their children's homework—typing papers, providing artwork, correcting math. The deal? The child doesn't have to work very hard, still gets good grades, and they all look good.

And what about those parents who think their gene pool should produce a professional athlete even though perhaps they themselves never excelled in sports? Have your children been on community-sports teams staffed by parent volunteers? While you've been grateful for the many hours given by these parent-coaches, doesn't it become painfully obvious at times that the reason for the volunteerism is not simply the love of the sport or children but rather, the parent-coach's desire to have his or her child be the star—the pitcher, the quarterback, or the soccer forward (whether Junior has the talent for the position or not)?

Every time their child hits a bump in the road, these same moms and dads are there, smoothing the path. Why? Because they believe their child is not capable of handling the situation alone. They are disloyal to their child's abilities. Every time the child sneezes, the youngster can count on his or her parents to be there to wipe the nose and clean up the messes. Why? Because Mom and Dad want to hide their perception of the child's inadequacy from the world.

So Mom and Dad write—oh, excuse me—type the term papers. Mom and Dad stay up all night working on the special projects. Homework is rarely a solo activity in these homes. I even know one mother who was upset because she wrote the paper that the teacher had the nerve to give her child a "B" for!

Some parents have so ignored the emotional boundaries between themselves and their children that they no longer understand where they stop and where their child begins.

COMMUNICATING DISAPPOINTMENT

When parents fail to respect the individuality of their children, seeing them primarily as extensions of themselves—well, then, the push is on. You see we've gotten to the point where being good in something isn't enough anymore. What we value is across-the-board achievement. It's not enough to be good in a couple of areas—we want straight A's and nothing less! We are disappointed when our children don't live up to the dreams we have for them. As a parenting culture, we are dangerously close to becoming disenchanted with the normal, average child. When we are disappointed with our children, when we are never satisfied with their performance, we are disloyal.

One psychiatrist explains the motivation behind such parent-child dynamics. "Parents who are disappointed with themselves and have felt lack of parental approval and acceptance are more likely to foster inappropriate expectations in their children. Unfortunately, we are the victims of victims and those of us who have been treated less than fairly often unfairly look to our children to redress wrongs inflicted on ourselves. This kind of vicarious living through children often makes for exorbitant expectations and even claims for perfection in various areas."[3]

TELLTALE SIGNS: BUMPER STICKERS AND BOOKS

Look at the societal signs. As a parenting culture are we living vicariously through the achievements of our children? Anybody have a bumper sticker on the family van that says something like, "We have an honor-roll student at Franklin Middle School?" What about a bumper sticker that proclaims superiority in other areas of life? Would you be insulted to read this on someone's car, "Our daughter is the prettiest girl at Central High" or "Our son is the best-dressed student at North High because his parents can afford it"? Is this harmless stuff? Why are we so insensitive to the salt we rub in the wounds of families whose children are less gifted academically? Because we're proud—proud at how all this genius reflects back on good old Mom and Dad!

When you think about it, wouldn't you just love to see this bumper sticker sometime?—"I am an average parent of an average middle-school student—and we're doing just fine!"

Frankly, a strong streak of narcissism is running through our culture's approach to family. What do I mean? My children are here to meet my needs! If our children can overachieve, it may remove the sting from the disappointment we feel with our own lives. If we're honest, we may find we are using our children to meet our own needs. We want our children to make us feel good about ourselves.

Look on the bookshelves of any bookstore. Scan through the titles—most of them could be subtitled—*How to Get Your Child to Be the Child You Want Him to Be! Help Your Child Realize His Potential!* the titles scream. *Increase Your Child's IQ!* Would you blink if you saw a book with this title, *Preparing for Harvard: A Guide for the First Two Years of Life?*

Well, as far as I know, there is no such book. But its spirit is certainly with us!

It's crucial that we parents understand what's at stake here. It's one thing for a child to experience interference from a parent over peas and bedtimes and clothing styles, but it's altogether another thing to experience controlling interference from a parent over *who you are*!

PARENTS WHO CROSS THE LOYALTY LINE

What if the primary message you received as a child was that you weren't good enough, not gifted enough, not smart enough, not attractive enough, that you were a big disappointment? What if your parents' lack of confidence in you was so strong that they never trusted you to handle your own life and experience your own consequences? What if you could never live up to the dreams your parents had for you?

Devastating! Worst of all, you might begin to perceive such parents as the "other side"— not "your side." You might come to see them as disloyal to who you are—the emotional enemy at home.

And that is the very message many children today are receiving from their overly ambitious, interfering parents. It is a message that is reinforced in this culture wherever a child turns.

Our children are bombarded with the pressure to work harder, excel more, be superstars in something if they are to matter at all. Too often, you are either a star, or you're a zero! This attitude pervades our educational system, our churches, our homes.

WHAT WE SHOULD BE APPLAUDING

Have you been to a high school graduation lately? Talk about psychological sadism! In the educational culture, only the very smartest are honored—and those few are honored over and over and over—ad nauseum. Average and above-average kids are subjected to that value system every day! Not only do they not get the 4.0 grade points, but they also don't receive the perks that come with being valued.

It's enough to break a kid's heart!

It broke *my* heart at our son's recent graduation.

Oh, our son had his share of perks, but fortunately his name wasn't mentioned to the point that everyone felt like throwing up at the sound of it! Having watched most of these kids grow up, I was offended that ninety-nine percent of them would have to sit through ceremonies designed to make them feel less valuable than other kids. This is a celebration? As my eyes scanned the blue-robed and mortar-boarded graduates, my heart went out to certain ones whose names were never mentioned for honor.

I saw Jeff. Here's a kid who's been in and out of mental hospitals throughout high school. It's not his fault—it's a combination of chemistry and home environment that he didn't choose. He has struggled to stay current with his class, wanting so much to be a part of them on graduation day. His diploma will be received after he completes some summer-school classes, but for now he marches with his friends. His life has been an enormous struggle to keep from drowning psychologically. But he is with his class today. It is a milestone in survival against the odds.

Someone should celebrate that kind of achievement!

I saw Gina. The first time we met her, her opening sentence was, "My parents are crazy. I was adopted by these people, and it was an enormous mistake! They are unfit parents." We thought she might be exaggerating, as kids are prone to do when the subject of parents comes up, but that night we learned of a grandmother locked in a bedroom, of Gina's fear of her father that drove her to find a boyfriend who could protect her physically against her father's abuse, of a mother so deranged she never touched Gina if she could help it. We were amazed at how quickly and easily she told her story to complete strangers. We never said it, but in our hearts we had to agree—how did the state allow these parents to have this girl? She is still an orphan—an emotional orphan! Gina's diploma would be a ticket out of a sick and abusive family system. I felt great pride for her as I watched her walk that day. This little bit of a girl had persevered against great hardship. She had beat the system!

Someone should celebrate that kind of achievement!

I thought of a face that was missing. Tewolde. He should have been there, but at Christmastime a drunk driver had taken his life. And what a life! The child of disabled refugees, and quite a gifted student, he had started his own cleaning business in order to support his family. Supporting one's family in high school can cut into extracurricular activities. There would be no sports or plays or clubs for Tewolde, but he never seemed bitter. In fact, just the opposite. Tewolde loved God. His heart was pure.

I will always regret that we didn't do more to help him. I didn't know how hard he was struggling—but I should have. But more than feelings of guilt, he's left his impression deep and tenderly on our memories. What a heart he had!

Someone should celebrate that kind of achievement!

I'm talking about average kids, below-average kids, all kids with special problems—but unique in their achievements because of them.

RAISING AN "AVERAGE" CHILD TO SUCCEED

You say your kid is just "average"? The report card is a disappointing collection of Bs, Cs and Ds. No teacher has ever glowed over your child. No coach has particularly wanted him or her on the team.

Then your role is obvious. Get over your own disappointment and be sure your child doesn't experience a double dose of heartbreak because Mom and Dad buy into such cruel values at home. It's a strong parent who can swim against the societal stream to make sure that his or her child feels accepted and delighted in. Regardless of what anyone else thinks. Be strong! Value your child! Be loyal!

HOW A PARENT'S LOYALTY HEALS

An incident from my childhood stands out to me. I had just entered junior high school. At that particular school, they grouped students according to academic ability. For the first time in my life I was taken out of a regular classroom and placed on an advanced track. I had been a straight-A student in grade school, but now I was competing for grades with thirty other "advanced" types. I was definitely the least of these. My grades dropped to Cs and Ds. My confidence dropped lower. Soon I developed strep throat and began to miss an inordinate amount of school.

Making matters worse, our homeroom teacher that year was the worst teacher I ever experienced in seventeen years of school! I dreaded her classroom and her humiliating, abusive approach to teaching. Boys were locked in utility closets for minor infractions—incompleted homework, for example. Girls were publicly embarrassed when answers were wrong. The stress was overwhelming. I remember crying a lot at night, not wanting my parents to hear me, sure that it was all my fault that life had taken this messy turn.

Enter my mother. I'll never forget how she steamed home after her parent-teacher conference with this toxic teacher. She reported that the woman felt that I was not really sick but running from my problems, that I was not smart enough to be in this particular class, that I was a girl who had been her male teachers' pet in grade school, which was the reason for my placement, not my native intelligence.

I thought the teacher was probably right. She was *the teacher*, after all. But my mother was not buying it! Putting the pieces together, she began to call other mothers only to discover that all the children, in this woman's opinion, were not qualified for the class, were grossly immature, given to cliquishness and irresponsibility . . . which is a perfect description of nearly all pubescent children, as anyone aware of child development would recognize.

No one could convince my mother that I was dumb. She loved my writing, my creative bent, my humor. She would not sit by and allow anyone to steal those things from me. To my great relief, she and my father stood by my side during that entire difficult year. They believed in me, they comforted me, they pumped up my damaged image. Under the circumstances, my Cs and Ds were accepted and understood. They didn't make me feel ashamed about being the dumbest of the smart, but they also didn't allow others to interpret me at the lowest possible denominator, either.

Amazingly, Mom also organized a parents' group that pressured the administration to terminate that particular teacher's position at our school. It was quite an astonishing thing, considering that my father was a college professor and that we generally operated within the framework of the teacher's always being right!

My parents were incredibly loyal to me during that difficult year. No one could ever convince them that I was stupid!

I can hardly tell you even today how pivotal my parents' deep support was in my healthy emotional development. My fragile, pubescent self-image took years to get over that particular teacher; I didn't begin to feel "semi-smart" again until college. But with my parents' deep belief in me, their stand-by-you-no-matter-what loyalty, I did recover.

MORE THAN UNCONDITIONAL ACCEPTANCE

The phrase "unconditional acceptance" is often used to describe how parents should relate to their children, but I also have a sense that acceptance alone will not do the trick in this day and age. It is too passive. Our culture is so psychologically damaging that acceptance alone will not undo everything that is done to our children.

Acceptance must be mixed with a large dose of something that, for lack of an appropriate word, I'll call *loyal delight* in who that child is. A parent's job is to celebrate the child, *as he or she is*. To be stood beside, even in tough times, is a secure feeling. Combine that with being enjoyed as a child, and you'll know what it is to belong. And there is little doubt that belonging is the central issue in many children's lives these days. If more parents would relax, back off the high-achievement track, stand by with loyal confidence—if more parents would express unshakable delight in who their child is—there would be so much less heartache in this world!

Back to my parents. They might have just "accepted" that I was becoming a C or D student, but they went further. No one could tarnish their view of me. I was special, and if my teacher didn't see it—then she must be blind!

> Acceptance must be mixed with a large dose of something that, for lack of an appropriate word, I'll call *loyal delight* in who that child is. A parent's job is to celebrate the child, *as he or she is*.

CHARACTERISTICS OF LOYAL PARENTS

This kind of parental loyalty, rooted in the acceptance and delight of the real child, has several facets. This is how one mental health worker wrote of parental loyalty:

1. Always respect the child's development and abilities. The child is not pushed beyond his or her capacity and not pressured to keep up with anyone else.
2. At all times, protect the child. Protection from outside forces of persecution or bigotry of any kind—antireligion, sexist discrimination, teachers who dislike redheads (or little girls who might have been their male teachers' "favorites"), or any ideas, concepts, or practices that are ultimately destructive.
3. Recognize, accept, and show appropriate patience with problems that come up. Problems are never treated in a rejecting, negative kind of way.
4. Never tolerate punishment in any form from a stranger! Children regard such a stance as uncaring, disloyal, and reflecting parental weakness.
5. Stand up to self-hate in the child whenever it is perceived. "I hate myself," or "I hate my looks," are statements that

    must be taken seriously and countermanded as quickly as possible.

6. See that the child gets appropriate praise and compensation relative to jobs and work done.

7. Be supportive and lend strength, wisdom, and compassion in times of need and crisis.

8. Avoid odious comparisons, especially with relatives or friends, or when the child participates in them in the service of self-hate. "John is a better player than me" should be countered with things they are good at and unique in.

9. Get help for the child when needed—especially if he or she requests it: medical help, counseling, therapy, teaching help, and so on.

10. Don't wait for the child to request help in more serious issues such as depression or excess anxiety.

11. Expect no more of your child than you do of yourself.

12. Never embarrass the child.

13. Don't admonish the child in front of other people.

14. Speak praise to him or her directly—not just to others.

15. Respect the child's secrets. Never trivialize his or her communications, however "cute" or childish they may seem to you.[4]

As I read that list I'm reminded of one word. *Loyalty.*

And what happens when a child fails to receive that kind of secure connecting with his parents? Well, take a real-life example. Recently I came across this account.

A Chilling Example

"When Lee Harvey Oswald, the man generally believed to have shot President John F. Kennedy, was a little boy, he and his older brother, Robert, were put in a boarding school. 'Lee wanted a normal family life,' Robert was to write. 'So did I, but I think I had already accepted the fact that our family was not like other families. . . .When parents of the other boys came to visit, I could see that their relationship with their sons was not at all like the relationship we had with our mother. Maybe because she had to worry about supporting us, she never had time to enjoy us. Other parents, it seemed to me, enjoyed their children. But we learned, very early, that we were a burden to her.'"[5] One can't help but wonder if history might have been rewritten if Lee Harvey Oswald had been a delight to his mother and had been given a sense of security and belonging.

Building Walls of Belonging

Do you want to drug-proof your child? Do you want to gang-proof your child? Do you want a child who reaches his or her potential? Do you want a child who can stay clear of sexual promiscuity? Many parents try a strict approach to achieve those goals. It often backfires into outright rebellion. Why not try attachment? Delight in that child! Communicate, "You matter! Your life matters!" Build the walls of belonging so deep around your child that the child will never be tempted to fill his or her life with any substitute that imitates acceptance and appreciation. Surround your child with your loyal devotion. Don't allow anyone to break that down.

WHAT DOES IT MEAN TO DELIGHT?

I like the concept of delighting in our children. It's the extra shine on the penny, the frosting on the cake, the handmade quilt that special effort has crafted. The dictionary defines *delight* in several ways.

- *A high degree of satisfaction*
  That means you forego the need to have your child be the most popular, the most talented, the most gifted. You express high contentment and gratification with exactly who your child is. Are you glad you had this child? Would you have traded her for any other? Why not tell her so?
- *To take great pleasure*
  Another way of saying this is to think of conveying the idea that your child has the power to make your day, your week, your life—that you *enjoy* being his or her parent.
- *To give keen enjoyment*
  Let your eyes light up when your children are around. Laugh more. Tell them how empty and quiet it is when they're not there. Enjoy the things they bring to your life. Attend their activities, not as if they were compulsories for parents, but throw yourself into their lives. Be a room mother, cheer at the ball games, open your home to their friends. *Enjoy, enjoy, enjoy!*

Say to your children through your words, your actions, your attitudes: You belong. At this house we are all weird in our own special ways—and without any reservations, without any doubts, with the greatest sense of satisfaction let us be sure that you know, now and forever—you belong!

It's a powerful truth.

> Let your eyes light up when your children are around. Laugh more. Tell them how empty and quiet it is when they're not there. Enjoy the things they bring to your life. Attend their activities, not as if they were compulsories for parents, but throw yourself into their lives.

RELATIONAL PRINCIPLE #4:
CHILDREN NEED PARENTS WHO ARE LOYAL TO AND DELIGHTED WITH THEM.

But why such an emphasis on delight? Isn't it enough to just love your child?

It all depends on what your child is perceiving.

Dr. Ross Campbell in his book, *How to Really Love Your Child*, described the gap that exists between our feelings of love for our children and what our children actually perceive, "It is a fact that most parents have a feeling of love toward their children. It is assumed, however, that parents naturally convey this love to a child. This is the greatest error today. Most parents are not transmitting their own heartfelt love to their children, and the reason is that they do not know how. Consequently, many children today to not feel genuinely, unconditionally loved and accepted."[6]

Do your children *feel* your love? Do they sense how much pleasure they give you? Do you laugh at their jokes, their stories, their friends? Do your children feel special *just the way they are?* Do they know how precious they are to you? Do they know you're glad you had them? Have you told them how well they're turning out? Do they sense that they make your day? Do you convey how great it is to spend time together? Does face light up when you see them? Do you drop everything to hear about their day, their thoughts, their feelings?

Remember, it is not enough that you *feel* loving. The test of your effectiveness as a parent is whether or not your child *perceives* that you love him or her. Does your child *feel* your love?

Want to know how to do that? Delight in your child!

A MOTHER'S PERCEPTION MATTERS

Actually there seems to be some self-fulfilling prophecy in the way parents view their children. If you feel your children are bright and delightful, they have a better chance of turning out that way. You might be interested in a study that tested the relationship between how mothers perceive their children and how the children actually turn out. Elsie Broussard developed a "neonatal perception inventory," a way to measure a mother's perception of her newborn's traits with those of other "average" infants. Broussard was then able to determine whether the mother viewed her own child as above or below average. She wondered, Would the mother's expectations for her child influence the child's future development?

When the babies became four and a half years old, they were evaluated by psychologists who had no idea of the mother's original feelings toward their children. Remarkably, the children they rated as superior turned out to be the ones initially rated as "above average" by their own mothers. The children who were behind or had psychological problems were also the ones whose mother's had viewed them originally as "below average."

At age ten, the children were retested by another set of psychiatrists who were also without prior knowledge, and the results were the same. The children whose mother's viewed them at birth as "superior" maintained a clear and significant advantage![7]

You can almost picture these mothers. It was "amazing" when their child learned to walk at about twelve months—not "average." Every lisped, baby word was cause for laughter and recorded in the baby book. Surely this was the stuff of genius! In a million ways the average stuff of life was transformed by the wonder in these mothers' eyes. No surprise these children became superior!

No matter if the night was filled with puking, the parent-teacher conference a disaster—these children could always come to their parents and with confidence feel, "Here I am, Mom! Here I am, Dad! Your bundle of joy!"

Your children deserve the advantage that comes from being delighted in and well-thought of!

A LESSON FROM A SPECIAL MOTHER

A while ago I watched a child coming home from school, and it occurred to me that we parents of "average" and "above average" kids could learn much from a certain segment of parents.

A special-education bus pulled up to a house near my parked car. From my car I watched the bus door swing open. Widely swinging arms and legs carefully and slowly made the descent. A little girl finally negotiated her landing, but one glimpse of her face told me she had other problems than coordination. She had Down's syndrome. She was also mentally challenged.

No sooner had she planted her feet on the curb than Mom came running from the house. It occurred to me that the end of the school day would mark the beginning of this woman's work day. I knew her real labor would start with the homecoming of this high-care child. But, her face was not weary looking, there was no apparent ambivalence about this moment. Charmingly, her arms opened wide, her face broke into a warm smile. A long embrace followed. This child of little potential was engulfed in welcome and love. She was her mother's delight! It wasn't hard to imagine, that this was their everyday ritual. It wasn't as if the hard work was beginning but as if the best part of the day had just begun!

As I've thought about that scene, as I've talked to parents of special-needs children, it has occurred to me that they have a great deal to teach the rest of us. Imagine it, with a doctor's diagnosis, all dreams for their child's future shatter. Self also dies. It's almost impossible to wear such a child as a trophy.

But along with the heartbreak, most of these parents would tell you, also comes a blessing. Parents of severely disabled children learn early the importance of unconditional acceptance. It's either accept the fact, or keep breaking your heart. A special-needs child holds a unique power in a parent's life. A shift takes place—away from achievement and accomplishment and competitiveness and pride—to living and breathing and sharing life and protecting the vulnerable and frail and innocent.

It is a heartbreaking gift—but a gift, just the same.

These parents with their children are also a gift to the rest of us. They model for the "average" world what unconditional love, acceptance, loyalty, and often pure delight of a child look like. They are among us for a reason.

If parents of "average" children could only make the same shift. If we only understood that on some level, each child is a special-needs child. It's as my son Justin wrote: "Everybody's weird in their own special way." Every person is a unique blend of the wonderful and the terrible. No two are even close to being the same.

These parents with their [special needs] children are also a gift to the rest of us. They model for the "average" world what unconditional love, acceptance, loyalty, and often pure delight of a child look like. They are among us for a reason.

We are the creation of God's hand, and it pleases him to populate the earth with the brilliant and the simple, the hunchback and the beauty queen. To the mix of the human race we bring our gifts and our deficits. Our children do, as well. We are an eclectic breed—it is part of our strange and terrifying beauty.

Acceptance of reality must displace our unrealistic parental dreams if we are to get to the place of loyally delighting in our children. I know—you wanted to raise a world-changer, a senator, a surgeon, or a great thinker—but the painful truth is that your son is so unfocused that it looks as though he's going to grow his hair in a ponytail and collect tickets at the roller rink.

It hurts.

WISE PARENTS' JOURNEY

But you can let go of your ideal and begin to appreciate the uniqueness of this particular child. It's an emotional journey that many a wise parent has learned to travel.

Many a parent has come to the fork in the road where reality separates from parental idealization, and has chosen the path of acceptance. That's being loyal on a deep emotional level. Add to that a delight factor and you have parents who understand that yes, their child may be weird—but also extremely special.

And when you and I achieve that kind of balance, of communicating loyal delight in our kids' potential—without pushing for the unachievable, of dreaming dreams for our children that are tempered with reality, of learning to celebrate the intrinsic child without enmeshed parental pride—well, someone should notice and celebrate that kind of achievement!

Parenthood symbolizes the end of childhood. To many, this begins the assumption of a role for which they are not emotionally equipped. Responsibility for a life other than their own overwhelms such parents. They feel incompetent or somewhat insecure themselves and find it difficult to cope with life themselves. They feel frightened when they imagine they must supply love and affection to another person.[1]

ROBERT W. FIRESTONE
Compassionate Child-Rearing

NINE

HEAT'S ON!

The Adult Parent

Do you remember this television commercial? A father sits on the top of a hillside, arm around his child. They are silhouetted in the glow of the sinking sun, which slowly disappears. Then, surrounded by the dark and an awesome silence, the child whispers, "Do it again, Daddy!"

Don't you love it?

Wouldn't it be wonderful if we could live up to the faith our young children have in us? We start out with everything on our side! Our babies think we are godlike. And then gradually our children must adjust their "bigger-than-life" view of us to reality.

This is a normal development in the parent-child relationship. By the time our children are grade schoolers, we have managed to convince most of them that we are plain, unawesome, not even close to perfect people.

> If we are to maintain a position of reasonable respect, it's important that we are more adult than our children.

I asked my oldest son when he realized that his parents were not all-powerful. He gave me a crooked smile, as if to say, "Oh sure, I never thought that about you—I was just putting you on." After some kidding around at my expense, he said he thought it was when he wanted a GI Joe and we said we didn't have the money. He was probably about three or four. Poor Brendan, child of our "hungry years," he learned the truth about his parents very early! His parents' powers were considerably limited!

There is so much we are not able to do for our children. We are restricted by our own resources. We are just human, not superhuman. Not that we would want our children to continue believing that we could make the sun set, but still, if we could just manage to keep one foot on the pedestal, easing our children into the truth, instead of crashing it down on them in a disillusioning heap.

If we are to maintain a position of reasonable respect, it's important that we are more adult than our children.

RELATIONAL PRINCIPLE #5: CHILDREN NEED PARENTS WHO ARE ADULTS.

For many children, the strong and compelling urge to live intimately with their parents is frustrated by their parents' immature behavior. Interfering parents, with their strong need to control, often sacrifice the obedience that would have come from their child's respect, for obedience that comes from domination.

Know any parents who are childish? Someone who can outdo the fireworks of any two-year-old temper tantrum? Ever seen a parental pouter, screamer, have-to-have-my-own-way-er, whiner, it's-always-the-other-guy's-fault-er, martyr, controller, manipulator, poor-me-er, complainer, fault finder, picky, self-centered, given to snits?

If the list seems slightly humorous, maybe it's because immaturity fits so incongruously on a parent. But it's the foolish, small stuff that eventually places many parents in their child's disdain.

THE BIG, BAD, BOSSY BABY PARENT

I recently came across an article titled, "How to Survive a Big Bad Boss." I was surprised at the similarities between bad executives and extreme control-oriented parents. That's because a child with an immature parent also has a "big bad boss!" I've kept the headings and defined them in terms of family. Under "Dominance-Oriented" came these characteristics:

1. Lack of control
   To the person who needs at all costs to dominate—yelling, screaming, tirades, tantrums all serve a useful purpose. It keeps the ones he or she wants to control intimidated and off-step emotionally.

2. Inappropriate behavior
   How about some public humiliation—like disciplining their children in front of their friends, or disciplining their children's friends? ("My child has made me mad—so you can all leave, NOW!—I don't care if I said I'd take you all swimming—or how far away you live, you can just walk home, the plans have been changed!")

3. Bluster, accusation
   The idea is, maybe these people won't notice when I screw up, if I can just keep the focus on *their* mistakes and shortcomings. The errors of other family members are overblown and given an inappropriate, overtly negative, emotional response. Everyone else in the family is interpreted at the lowest possible denominator. However, should anyone dare to point out Mom's or Dad's blunders—well, watch out! The door of criticism used by such parents is only allowed to swing one way!

4. Scheming, wheedling
   A bad boss who uses this method to dominate others is an expert at guerrilla tactics to get his or her way. He or she is always a step ahead in planning the next strategy.
   In a home setting, this personality operates by covertly pitting family members against each other. It's all under the table, but should the family members ever trust each other enough to compare notes—well, it would be most revealing!

5. False charm
   No one outside the family can believe that things can be as bad as is being described. Mom and Dad seem so "nice." Too nice—if you think about it. It's a cover-up for a lack of

real feeling for other people. It's frosting on a dill pickle! Unfortunately in time, everyone who gets close will experience the real person behind the charming, altruistic, volunteer-for-the-PTA-type parent. It explains why, if you look closely at such parents, there is usually a lack of long-term adult friends.

6. Self-esteem from superiority
   The parent doesn't feel comfortable if anyone else experiences success. It makes him or her feel less like "top dog" to have anyone else shine.

7. Conflict, endless arguments, squabbles
   There is little emotional energy left over for healthy pursuits. The family's emotional resources are used in coping and surviving life with this stressful peace-breaker.

8. Self-pity
   Because by definition these parents operate with a limited emotional development—we can expect them to be a real wah-wah about their own lives. Others' feelings are immaterial—what really matters is how *they* are feeling. Their feelings are expected to be the focus of family attention, and they are also the negative hook by which other family members are controlled. To diffuse the anger, family members learn to say in various ways, "Poor Mommy. Poor Daddy" even if inside they are totally repulsed by the parents' immaturity and self focus.

9. Invasion of boundaries
   This can be both a physical and emotional trespass. Again, such parents operate with the framework that their child exists to meet their needs: Therefore, if I need to know what's going on in your life, I read your mail, snoop in your room, and eavesdrop on your phone conversations. And if I believe you exist to make me feel good about myself, I can make emotional demands on your life because I am your parent.

10. Deaf to facts
    Reality is unimportant. Don't even bother. What matters to such a parent is how he or she feels. So the child missed curfew because he or she was in a near-fatal accident.

There is still a tirade at home because Mom and Dad were subjected to worry and stress.

11. Irrational, senseless

Living with an adult child can make anyone feel as though he is losing his mind. So much makes no sense at all.

12. Morass

Funny, but this is exactly as it sounds! It's a dedication to and consistent taking of the emotional low ground. It's living in an emotional bog of negativity, smallness, and self-centeredness.[2]

WHERE DOES A KID GO TO COMPLAIN?

The advice given to employees of such immature bosses is simple—complain to higher management, keep a record should you decide to sue, or quit if you can.

But what if you are a child with a big bad boss? There's usually no higher authority to complain to, you can't sue your own parents (although some children have recently taken their case against their parents to court), or quit your family. What do you do?

If you're desperate, you might do what one teenage boy did recently. He killed his parents. His explanation? Had he been subjected to physical or sexual abuse? Yes. But his biggest complaint was emotional abuse. Note how he described life with a big, bad baby father.

"My dad abused me and my brother when we were younger. He was alcoholic, and he put my mother through twenty years of [expletive]. I didn't want to see my mom suffer anymore. My father beat me until I was fourteen years old and continued to nag and push us all around. 'Clean this up, clean that up.' He started this stuff with me and my brother and our mother. 'This isn't done, that isn't done.' Little things like that, and he made a big deal out of them. If you left a cup downstairs, he would be after you. But if he did it, well that was all right. He told Mom he didn't go out to the bars, but I would see his van there. We wouldn't dare tell Mom the truth. . . ."[3]

It's rough having a big, bad, bossy baby for a parent.

Immature parents are not all murdered, thank heaven, but many of them eventually experience total emotional distance from their children.

BIG, BAD, BOSSY PARENTS DON'T LAST FOREVER

I remember a wedding in Florida that my husband, Steve, and I participated in. Steve performed the ceremony, and I sang. The tension behind the scenes was excruciating. Big, bad baby father did not approve of the marriage. He threatened to boycott the affair by not attending. I'll never forget the pain the bride experienced on the day that should have been the happiest of her life. Tears rolled down her cheeks. The anxiety over whether or not she would have a father to walk her down the aisle was almost unbearable for her. At the last second—literally as the organ started "Here Comes the Bride!"—he blew in. A phoney smile plastered his face. He looked like the loving father. The bride graciously and maturely allowed him to take his place of honor by her side. No one in the congregation had a clue about the emotional torture to which he had subjected his sweet young daughter. I thought then, with amazement, that this rascal had gotten away with it.

And he might have, had this been his only blunder. If the pre-ponderance of evidence had pointed to his maturity, not to his immaturity, he probably would have been forgiven even for this. But as this family story has unfolded over the past fifteen years, big, bad baby father has managed to make everyone miserable with his demands and self-centered immaturity. "Morass," you might say! It's interesting to note that the "unapproved" marriage has survived, but the father-daughter relationship hasn't; at its best, it's characterized by tolerance, avoidance, and resentment. Eventually, he didn't get away with it. He lost what he cared about most—his daughter.

But, before I come down too hard on immature parents, let me ask, Have you noticed, as I have, how hard it can be to be mature?

WHEN THE HEAT'S ON, BEWARE THE TACTICS YOU USE

Confession. I, too, have behaved less than maturely at times. Especially when the heat's been on. Let me share one incident to diffuse any unnecessary guilt you might be feeling right now.

I like to think that our family is very close. I want to think that my children think I'm a wonderful mother, because I definitely am moti-vated to be that. And so, when I am occasionally the object of criticism—it kind of hits me where I live emotionally.

Here's the scenario—an example of "ungrace" under pressure. We were driving home from a wonderful Thanksgiving holiday with extended family. I had worked very hard at food preparation and making the arrangements for the family to be together. I had been charming at times when I might have been otherwise. I thought my family should notice.

I fished. "Does anyone have anything to say about our weekend?" I opened the door for warm comments and grateful words. And then he said it. My son. The one who is the most like me.

"Mom, I don't feel like you take me seriously! When I tell you my ideas, you always counter with the opposing position. I really don't think you're listening to me."

What was this? I really didn't get it.

"What are you talking about?" I questioned, "Give me an example."

"Well, it happened this weekend. I said to you, 'I think those animal-rights activists are a bunch of idiots,' and right away you said, 'Well, the animals are helpless to protect themselves, they would be taken advantage of if people didn't defend them.' (I'm thinking, *So this is my big crime?*)

"Mom, I just wish that once you wouldn't come right back with *the right answer*. You kind of assume that I'd said something incredibly dumb instead of finding out why I said what I said."

At this point I was dangerously close to becoming an unsafe parent —one who is so thick she never catches on to what her children are trying to say. A burning feeling was rising in my throat. The feeling that convinces me I am misunderstood—a woman living in a boys' club. They are so thick with each other, these men in my family, they don't understand women at all.

Enter, Baby Mom!

With a tinge of chilling superiority in my voice I countered with, "Well, Son, how do you expect me to respond if you're going to say something so dumb?"

"Mom, that's my point exactly. I wish you would respond with something like—well, 'That's an interesting viewpoint, why do you say that?' Don't just assume that I'm young and don't have anything to say!"

He was not backing down. *Oh, brother, just what I can't tolerate*, I thought. *Male ego. He wants me to worship at his little male shrine.* This was really nasty. I remembered that this son had been beginning many of his statements and questions in our home with "Dad, what do you think?" or "Dad, I forgot to tell you about . . ." or "Dad, guess what happened today?" even when Mom and Dad were both in the room. Lately, I had been noticing that it was like I wasn't even there.

This male bonding has gone too far in this family! This guy thing, this exclusionary misunderstanding of the female perspective has gone too far! I would cut it off at the pass.

"How small can you be? Maybe you'd like to go live with (the name of a friend whose mother is a *real* shrew), then you'd really have grounds for complaint. You have it so good. What nerve you have to be so picky about such a small thing! And while we're being truthful, why don't you ever complain about your father? He's not perfect, you know! If I practiced this kind of favoritism between you and your brother, you would really be hurt—and I *am*!"

To make my point, I didn't say another word all the way home. My anger turned to silent tears, and I was unconsolable. I pouted, in other words.

It's rough being a big, bad, bossy baby parent!

I felt awful. I felt like pond scum. My son was convinced that I *was* pond scum!

I had nuclear-bombed our family trust bank with my inappropriate level of emotional reaction. It was days before I could undo this situation with my son and sit down to talk with the purpose of understanding, not necessarily defending.

What was the issue? He wanted me to see him as a man, not just as my little boy. It's a natural developmental stage that boys——oops!— men his age pass through. (I'm still working on this.) He wanted to sense that his mother, the most important woman in his life to this point, thinks he's smart and insightful and worth listening to! (Of course I do believe all these things about him—I just wasn't communicating it in the way he could hear it.) He was doing the hard work of individuating— particularly from me—the one whom he most closely resembles. He needed to separate and find himself. I was not helping the process.

My point: Even adults who have the nerve to write books about relating to children can behave like babies. Especially when we're tired, especially when the heat's on.

In some situations it's very hard to be adult!

But it is precisely when the heat is on, when we are the victims of misunderstanding or criticism that seems small or unfair, that we have the opportunity to show that we really are adult and therefore trustworthy.

IN INTENSE MOMENTS, PARENTS NEED A BATTLE PLAN TO FIGHT FAIRLY AND MAINTAIN ADULT DIGNITY

When the heat's on, a parent will lose his or her adult positioning and become foolishly childish unless committed to some basic relational principles for tough times. Here's some guidelines to help keep your parental self behaving as an adult.

1. COMMIT TO NON-ESCALATION.

   If our child has set a low tone—we will not match, or in my case, set an even lower pitch. If I could relive that situation (and I'm sure I'll have other opportunities to try again!) I would try to listen without exacerbating the discussion with an overly emotional or threatened response. For instance, instead of reacting emotionally (as if personally threatened) to my son's criticism, I would have appeared less foolish if I had right then dug to the root of what he was trying to communicate to me.

2. ACCEPT OUR PARENTAL ROLE WITHOUT RESENTMENT OR EXPECTATION OF UNDUE PRAISE.

   If we felt uncared for in our own childhoods, or if we hold to idealized concepts about being a parent, we may find ourselves harboring ambivalent feelings of resentment when the parental job gets demanding and seems to be more than we bargained for.

   Being a parent calls for sacrifice at nearly every turn. Our resources—financial, emotional, time, energy—can be totally drained by one hard day of parenting. It's true. Parenting can be a real drag! And to make matters worse, kids have a maddening way of taking totally for granted the daily sacrifices of their parents.

   On the one hand, if you expect praise for food on the table and clean clothes in the drawers, if you believe your children should rise up and call you blessed because you provide a home and care for them daily, you will be very disappointed. Being a parent is the most taken-for-granted role you may ever have. Kids don't usually understand what it costs you to care for them until they become parents themselves. Then they may "get it."

On the other hand, this also makes way for enormous sacrifice to be noticed. Situations that call for noticeable sacrifice are really opportunities to do something that gets your child's attention. For instance, I'll never forget the forest-green velvet gown my mother stayed up all night to make for me when I, at the last minute, got a solo part in a performance of the Messiah at my college. Poor Mom slept through most of the performance, but I felt so loved—and I noticed. Not only did I notice, I remember because of that instance, that even though Mom is gone now, I was a loved child.

What's the point? Do the daily sacrifices without blowing a trumpet or hoping for any special notice.

And when the opportunity comes to build a model of the Eiffel Tower in one night, to host the New Year's Eve party that no other parent in his right mind wants—go for it! That kind of sacrifice will sink in and be noticed and also *remembered* through the years as part of your love legacy!

3. ABANDON THE ATTITUDE OF "I AM THE PARENT, THEREFORE I AM RIGHT!"

   Only people living totally in the dark believe they are always right. You are not in the dark. Listen to what your children are trying to say. Try to understand; they may be right! Even if they're not right, you need to hear and understand their perspective.

4. LEARN TO DIG.

   That means that we ask clarifying questions until we get to the bottom line. Don't trust your initial reaction to your child's criticism. Don't make a response based on their initial words. Children have difficulty expressing their feelings verbally—especially in the face of an intimidating adult. Ask questions that help you understand how your child feels. It doesn't matter if the approach or reasoning seems irrational—find out what's going on beneath the words. Dig until you find and understand their point of pain or frustration with you.

5. COMMIT TO CHANGE AND SELF-IMPROVEMENT.
Be glad that someone cares enough about a relationship with you that he or she is willing to help you improve. Ask your child to point out and remind you when you're "doing it again."

6. LEARN TO SAY THOSE MAGICAL, ADULT, RELATIONAL WORDS, "I'M SORRY!"
When we apologize, we admit that the relationship with our child is more important than being right or having our hurt feelings noticed. Apologizing says, "You matter more to me than anything else, including my pride."

This is the stuff of adulthood. It's the mature approach.

GOD IS CUSTOM-MAKING YOU INTO THE PARENT YOUR CHILDREN NEED

Much is made in family literature of the development of the child, but family life is a two-way street. Living together as a family is meant as much for the refinement, maturation, and development of the parent as for the child. It is a wise and eventually well-loved parent who will allow her children to rub off some of their rough edges, to feed back about some of their immature areas, to go toe-to-toe over issues that need addressing. Your goal is to become the custom-made parent for your particular child.

Children are God's way of stimulating spiritual, emotional, and relational growth in parents. Pay attention. You thought that becoming a good parent was about child management, but through your children, God is still forming the man or woman he intends for you to become. For the sake of relationship with our children, some of us will be motivated as we never were before, to become safe, whole, and mature.

It's a great system—if we will submit to it and grow!

Children are God's way of stimulating spiritual, emotional, and relational growth in parents.

ATTENTION! LITTLE LEANS ON BIG FOR STRENGTH

There is one last area that needs to be mentioned when we talk about being adult and mature as parents. It's this matter of leaning. Who is leaning on whom? In every relationship someone gives more, someone listens more, someone is called into understanding and acceptance of the other person to a greater degree. In the parent-child relationship, this is the parent's role. The child should never be put in the role of being the strong tower, the caretaker, the nurturer of an immature parent.

One person described the maturity of his parents in this way, "My parents knew how life should be conducted. They had confidence in the choices they were making, and they made us feel that we should have confidence, too. To this day I can't stand to see parents wrestling over the macaroni of their lives in front of the child. My parents must have had some tough decisions to make, but I was never called on to bear witness to their anxiety. To some people that might sound like repression, but I think repression can be a positive value."[4] I believe he makes an important point. There was no inappropriate emotional leaning in this family! There was no blurring of the lines over who were the parents and who were the children. The parents took responsibility without whining, without being overly anxious—they provided a secure beginning for their children simply by their maturity.

This was an issue in my home when I was growing up. My mother was a working mom. Her mother, my grandmother, often helped us out by coming over to clean and organize when my mother got behind. This was all great, except she tended to have the attitude of, "Why aren't you children keeping this house clean?" We were in grade school. I always thought that was somehow twisted. At least, I don't remember being particularly responsive to that approach. (Life does have some poetic justice, however. Somewhere in heaven, Mom and Gram are having the last laugh—I am now living in my mother's house and get to take care of it—ALL BY MYSELF!)

Let's be clear about this. Children are not there to cook, clean, and launder for the adults. Neither are they to be our counselors. Nevertheless, in many households if these things are to happen at all, the child must do them. Learning responsibility and having some chores is very different from bearing most of the responsibility. Teaching a child to do her share is very different from expecting her to do the lion's share. Not only are these inappropriate expectations, but usually the child understands that she is being used and comes to greatly resent such role reversals.

No child should be expected or required to parent, take care of, nurture, his or her own parents.

Attention! Little leans on big for strength! That's the way it's designed to work. There may come a day when you and I are old and feeble, perhaps even senile, when our roles will be reversed and we will need to lean on our children, but during these family years, the leaning needs to be done by the young on the old. In these years, leaning is done from the bottom up!

MAKE YOUR KIDS PROUD

There is an interesting verse tucked in Scripture that puts a twist on the parent-child relationship. Most Scriptures emphasize the importance of the child's behavior in the relationship. For instance, "A sensible son gladdens his father. A rebellious son saddens his mother" (Proverbs 15:20 LB). Or, "A wise youth accepts his father's rebuke; a young mocker doesn't" (Proverbs 13:1 LB). Those are familiar verses, but I like this one precisely because of the spin it puts on our normal perspective about raising children: "Parents are the pride of their children" (Proverbs 17:6b).

Hmm . . . Interesting.

What does it mean? Several things. It means that your well-lived life is a blessing to your child. Your child can enjoy the reflected glow from your reputation and wisdom. It means when you turn away from the childish need to dominate, the foolish need to control, excessive emotional leaning, and all other behavior that belittles you and your family, your child will respect you.

More than that: Through the years, you just may find yourself becoming your son or daughter's great pride and joy—the stuff of family legend and endearing anecdote.

It means that you will become the object of your child's love and respect, the basis of relationship for a lifetime.

Go ahead. Take the high, adult road. Become the pride and blessing of your children's' lives. Submit to the discipline. And then listen. What do you hear in the awesome silence? Your child's voice is speaking. *Do it again, Dad. Do it again, Mom. Work the miracle again. Show us once more how it is we grow up and become adult.*

*I will try to walk a blameless path, but how I need your help,
especially in my own home where I long to act as I should.*

PSALM 101:2 TLB

TEN

NOT PERFECT BUT PRESENT:

*Quality Time
and the Available Parent*

Until now I have been forbidden by my two teen-age live-in "censors" to share the stories you are about to read. For years, these episodes from their lives have been deep-sixed from public life. They refused me permission to let them pass even from my lips to the ears of my nearest and dearest friends. It has something to do (so they say) with not enjoying being publicly embarrassed.

This attitude has presented me with quite a dilemma. You see, I knew, even while these incidents were in process, even while my emotions were fully engaged, I knew, deep inside, even then—that a GREAT illustration was in the making. As a communicator, my typical attitude is, What's a little public humiliation if a memorable point can be made? I tell embarrassing things about myself all the time!

My sons do not share that same perspective.

But, fortunately, enough time has passed that even they can now laugh at themselves in these situations. I was given, however, one stipulation. I must share equally about each of them. So although one illustration would do, you'll have to wade through two stories, for the sake of fairness.

Fortunately for you, we don't have ten children!

For several months of the year, my husband's work involves a great deal of traveling. So while he jets around, I try to keep the functioning side of our lives intact. It is a small taste of what single parenting must be like. *How do these single moms and dads do it alone?* I always find myself wondering. At our house, we depend on Steve to keep our lives in functioning order, as I am not a person who is highly gifted, or actually even slightly gifted, in the area of organization. Unfortunately, details are just something that fall through the cracks when I'm the sole parent on duty, so I'm never too sure if all the misadventures that happen to us while Steve's gone are because he's not with us, or because I am the adult who is present.

All I know is that when I parent alone—stuff happens!

Turning Forty! A Disaster without Dad!

Thankfully, we usually have two parents to keep things ordered! In our household, two parents are not an option, they're a necessity!

For instance, let me tell you about the day I turned forty. It was a cold, blustery November morning. I don't know whether it was the milestone, or the weather, but it was the kind of morning when staying in bed was an inviting but, unfortunately, impossible option.

It was piano-lesson morning. That meant both boys had to be separately chauffeured to Mrs. Clark's house at an inhuman before-school hour. First, Brendan would be dropped off, and immediately the car would be driven right back home to pick up Justin. Then usually, by the time Justin and I drove back to Mrs. Clark's, Brendan was done with his lesson and needed to be dropped off at middle school. Finally, the car headed back to Mrs. Clark's for the third time and picked up and deposited Justin at grade school. For this schedule to work, it had to be executed with to-the-second timing.

That's how most piano mornings go.

But not this one.

Just as Justin and I were backing out of our driveway, I remembered that it was garbage-collection day. "Justin, quick, help me get the cans to the curbside so we won't be late to your lesson. Work fast, and we'll still be able to get you and Brendan to school on time!" Hoping to take only a minute and wanting to keep the car warm, we closed our doors, and I left the keys in the ignition with the motor running.

I had not counted on my son's efficiency. He had power-locked his door, and now we were locked both out of our home and our running car. The father and, more important, his extra set of keys, were in Canada. It was time to be resourceful.

Ordering Justin to keep an eye on our car, I ran to a neighbor's, several houses down the block, and called Mrs. Clark. I explained our dilemma and asked her to drive Brendan to school. She was understanding. No problem. Next, I called the police, who must be old hats at breaking into locked cars. Surely, they could help us. In no time, a police officer was in our driveway. He really did try to help us but was unable to unlock our door, fearing he might ruin the electrical wiring for the window. We were still locked out! Oh, no, now what?

"Call your car dealer, lady. They can make you a new key."

Back to the neighbor's house. "May I use your phone again, please?" When he answered the phone, the dealer explained we needed a number from the dashboard. Did I have it?

No. Back to our house.

There was our car, just as I'd left it, billowing exhaust on this cold autumnal morning. But, where was Justin? I called his name. No answer. A panicky thought crossed my mind. Had someone kidnapped him? How stupid could I be to leave a little boy guarding a car all by himself! I should have let someone take our car and kept my eye on Justin!

I began to search. I walked around the house. My heart was pounding. No Justin! Maybe he was in the garage. Maybe he had gone there to try to stay warm. I opened the garage door. I called his name.

No answer. But, I could see breath rising from behind a bin. "Justin, is that you? Are you hiding?"

"I'm here, Mom," his little voice responded. With enormous relief, I walked over to the rising breath. There he was! But his face was sad, his eyes teary.

"What in the world is the matter? Sweetheart, this isn't worth getting upset over."

"Mom, I think you might think it's worth getting upset over when I tell you what I did while you were at the neighbor's. You know that TV show, *McGyver*, where he fixes things with whatever he has?"

"Yes?" I say. But inside I'm thinking, *Oh, no!*

"Well, if you look in the driver's-side keyhole, you'll find the handle of my jacket zipper. I thought maybe I could unlock it, but instead it broke off in the lock. Now, you can't even unlock it with a key! Plus, my jacket is broken."

Steve, where are you when I need you?

By noon all our problems had been solved. A new key had been made. The lock was unjammed. Justin was back in school. In all, it had been a four-hour ordeal.

And I was exhausted. Turning forty was a drag! I put myself to bed, covered my head with blankets, and put an end to a "Terrible, horrible, no good, very bad day!"

At such times I'm convinced that God was incredibly smart when he designed a family with two parents! We all need a back-up system when "stuff" starts happening.

Brendan's Excellent Adventure

Why do these things always happen when Steve's away? Several summers ago the boys and I decided to extend our family vacation by a week. We stayed on in a cabin at the edge of the wilderness in the mountains of North Carolina, while Steve returned to work without us.

As far as our boys are concerned, there is no greater adventure than riding a dirt bike on a primitive mountain trail, but at that time the house rules were clear: Every hour they were to report back home. This kept them within a certain radius for safety, and in case they ran out of gas, they were still within walking distance to the cabin.

On this particular day, only Justin, our youngest, came back on the hour. He explained that Brendan had gone off into the wilderness with three other motorcyclists.

"Kids?" I asked.

"No," he reported sheepishly. "I'd say they were about thirty years old!"

"What?" I frantically called Steve. I explained the situation. "We've told him not to get into cars with strangers. We've told him to be careful in a million different ways. But I never thought to warn him about going into the wilderness with people he doesn't know."

"Steve, what should we do?"

"I don't know!" he said, "I'm hundreds of miles away! Try not to worry, he'll probably show up soon."

"Well, why are you *always* hundreds of miles away when these things are happening?" With visions of Jeffrey Dahmer flooding my mind, I raced in my van to the isolated area where the trails began. I followed the trail on foot as far as I humanly could. I called out his name. Panic took over reasoning. I put big rocks on the floor in the front of our van and waited to defend my son against whatever I might find when these wilderness motorcycle men came back to their truck. I was a mother ready to die to protect her son. I wrote down their vehicle description and their license numbers and watched and waited. Several times I retraced the trail, calling Brendan's name.

I waited for four excruciating hours.

When he finally came down the trail with his new friends, he was extremely fortunate to survive the reunion with his mother!

His explanation? He had been led deep into the wilderness and realized that he had no way of finding his way back down unless he also descended with his "new friends." To avoid becoming lost, he had no choice but to stay with them, on their time schedule.

Before I could even think of an appropriate response, God intervened. At least it seemed so at the time. Brendan was complaining about being a "little itchy."

And he was a "little itchy" in a most private place. While up in the mountains, he explained, they had stopped for a break. He had relieved himself in some bushes. A bit later his skin began feeling hot and scratchy. He broke out in a rash. *Everything* in the jockey-short area turned a blazing purple color. He was miserable! As it turned out, the pharmacist verified that the "bush" had actually been poison oak! For the rest of the week, he suffered with the worst case of jock itch on human record!

It was punishment enough. We sometimes get what we thoroughly deserve!

THE BALANCE OF THE TWO-PARENT SYSTEM

It feels like these things only happen when Dad's away, but the truth is, when I parent alone, my emotional resources are depleted and I overreact. Instead of a responding parent, my children are left to deal with an overreacting parent who is going over the edge. It's my highly emotional response to these daily life experiences that make them stand out in my mind as parenting days from hell. And the point is, a hard day of parenting for Mom often becomes an even harder day for her kids.

Two parents provide emotional balance for each other. As I think about it, things happen when Steve's home, too. But when he's not there to calm and reassure me that everything will be okay, I can easily lose perspective. (I provide this same balance for him when his emotions are engaged and things seem blown out of proportion.) Children need the perspective of the emotionally nonengaged parent to help them through situations when one parent is overreacting emotionally.

My main point is that children need the stability provided by two parents who can balance each other out. Even if there has been a divorce or separation between the parents, in most cases, children need the emotional engagement of both parents. Once we become parents, we need to be committed to being available to them. Unfortunately, the statistics point to the fact that many children are also being divorced from one of their parents when the marriage does not work out. Increasingly, we are acquiring hard evidence that points to the difficulty our children have in a one-parent-system.

Did you know that:

- "One million children go through divorce or separation every year?
- Only fifty percent of American children can expect to spend their entire childhood in an intact family?
- Contrary to popular belief, children of divorce 'do worse' than children in intact families on several measures of well-being?
- Children in single-parent families are six times as likely to be poor? They are also likely to stay poor longer. Twenty-two percent of children in one-parent families will experience poverty during childhood for seven years or more, compared with only two percent of children in two-parent families.
- A 1988 survey by the National Center for Health Statistics found that children in single-parent families are two to three times as likely as children in two-parent families to have emotional and behavioral problems? They are also more likely to drop out of high school, to get pregnant as teenagers, to abuse drugs, and to be in trouble with the law.
- Research also shows that many children from disrupted families have a harder time achieving intimacy in a relationship, forming a stable marriage, or even holding a steady job."[1]

To these frightening statistics we must add the reality that many American kids' fathers abdicate their roles. In an article entitled, "A Missing Father Can Create a Void That Can't Be Filled," Ellen Goodman points out that "Today, about one-third of all American children—nineteen million—live away from their fathers. Among the children of divorce, half have never visited their father's home. In a typical year, forty percent of them don't see their father. Twenty percent haven't seen their father in five years."[2]

The article continues by quoting David Blankenhorn of the Institute for American Values: "Today's favorite image may be that of the 'new father,' but the real direction is toward fatherless children. This is the most socially consequential fact of our era."[3]

All the facts point to the alarming truth. In single-parent families, when one adult shoulders sole responsibility, too often "stuff" happens! My yearly seasonal taste of single parenting has convinced me that these statistics are true.

Almost more than anything else, children need parents committed to "being there." They don't need perfect parents, but they do need parents who are present.

RELATIONAL PRINCIPLE #6:
CHILDREN NEED TWO PARENTS WHO ARE AVAILABLE.

This simple need of children is one of the hardest for many parents to meet. Our culture is moving away from parents' "being there." Being there is in direct conflict with so many of the adult world's priorities.

How much time do parents really need to be there? One societal concept that is often bantered about is this one of "quality time." The idea is that it isn't how *much* time is spent with a child, but the *kind* of time that matters to children. Unfortunately, many parents have interpreted that to mean that a trip to Disney World, or shopping for an expensive piece of clothing, maybe an outing to purchase a new bike or stereo, will compensate for the many hours of separation on a day-to-day basis.

Not true! If you want to spend quality time with your child, you need to be available WHEN THEY NEED YOU. Quality time, by definition, is not possible on a per perk basis—a weekend here, a vacation there. Quality time is being available on an "as needed" basis. Quality time is the consistent daily sharing of life with your children. *Quality time is the time spent in meeting your child's needs.*

WHAT DOES QUALITY TIME LOOK LIKE?

- Quality time is experienced when a child needs help with homework and you are there.
- Quality time is volunteering to be the room mother, or a chaperone for a field trip.

- Quality time is when a child can't sleep at night and you're available to pray over him or her, comforting and soothing your child's anxieties.
- Quality time is Mom and Dad sitting in the bleachers, cheering enthusiastically even if their kid rarely gets to play in the game.
- Quality time is watching TV and holding hands.
- Quality time is walking together in the evening and talking about dreams for the future.
- Quality time is when your kid has friends over and you're around to enjoy them.
- Quality time is working on a project at home together.
- Quality time is laughing at each other's jokes.
- Quality time is going to the movies together and pigging out on "Twizzlers" and popcorn.
- Quality time is eating a cozy, uninterrupted meal together, sharing the details of ordinary days.
- Quality time is sharing with each other the things you're reading.
- Quality time is shared life—not just occasional perks.
- Quality time is getting to know your child so well that you can anticipate and meet his or her needs.
- Quality time is arguing over a point until you each understand the other's point of view better.

The facts are—many parents are missing out on their children's childhoods. It's not just in homes of divorce that parents can be missing. There are so many ways we can miss "being there." We can be distracted, emotionally aloof, or unavailable. Many are even geographically distanced. In some cases, it's very difficult to stay involved. I understand that sometimes noncustodial parents feel that they have been driven out of their children's lives. But, if you understand that one of your child's greatest needs is YOU, and if you care for your child, then you should do everything humanly possible to "be there."

> The facts are—many parents are missing out on their children's childhoods. It's not just in homes of divorce that parents can be missing. There are so many ways we can miss "being there."

Our public debate has centered around how much time parents can be away from their children without damaging them. Isn't it interesting that we're willing to settle on debate around survival and keeping damage to the minimum when we speak of our children? That is not what we're talking about. We're speaking about *what your children need from you in order to feel close and attached and secure with you*—not how little you can give them and still have them survive emotionally. There is a big difference!

What if you find yourself "home alone" as a single parent? Can you help your family avoid becoming part of the alarming statistics. Absolutely! Your best protection against the trends is building strong relationships with your children.

And, you will have one additional hurdle to jump. You already realize that one of your biggest frustrations is finding the time and energy to enter into shared life. There is only one of you for a two-person job. You will probably find it a stretch just to keep things functioning. All the more reason that you will need to be careful that with your limited time and resources your child doesn't come in last in your priorities.

Most important, you need to take care of yourself so that you have something to give your children. If *your* well is empty, you will not be able to meet anyone else's needs very well.

GUARDING YOUR EMOTIONAL RESOURCES

Here are some suggestions that can help.

1. Simplify your life. Don't try to live at the same level you did when only two adults were managing the house. Learn to downscale and simplify. Most single parents are forced to live with less, but don't think of it as a loss but as something you do for yourself to help your lives be less complicated. These years are too precious, your children too dear, for you to be the caretaker of the wrong details.

2. Because your time is limited, share the workload with your kids. Don't just divide and conquer the things that need to be done. You'll end up with all going separate ways in the evenings instead of being together. Work on chores *together*. While you're folding the laundry together, find out how things are going with your child and his or her best friend. Cook together and find out how that tough

class is going, or who the current love-of-their-life is. Make chore time relational time as well.

3. Don't try to do it all. Choose time well-spent with your children over clean houses, home-cooked meals, or whatever. Refuse to feel guilty if things don't look like *Better Homes and Gardens* at your house, especially if it's because you have chosen to use your time and energy "being there" for your children.

4. If you are divorced, and your "ex" can be trusted (I didn't say, "liked," —I said, "trusted"—in terms of your children), encourage his or her involvement in your children's lives. You need the back-up help.
Your children need his or her attention and involvement. Sometimes this is an enormous pill to swallow, but if you have the grace, swallow the pill for the sake of civility and the best interests of the children.

5. If you are a noncustodial parent, don't divorce your children as well. Abandoned children are vulnerable to meeting their father-hunger in a myriad of frightening and unhealthy ways. They may try to fill the father-gap and the mother-need with substitutes, but the truth is: *No one can replace you.* You are so important to your children. Don't move away! Don't try to replace and forget them with a "new family." Stay connected!

All parents need to be involved at a level that allows them to get to know their constantly evolving child. Try this experiment. It's fun! Answer the following questions. Have your son or daughter write out their answers separately and then compare notes.

HOW WELL DO YOU KNOW YOUR CHILD?

1. Who is your child's best friend?
2. What color would he or she like her bedroom to be?
3. Who is his or her hero?
4. What embarrasses him or her?
5. What is your child's greatest fear?
6. What is his or her favorite music?
7. What person outside the family has most influenced your child?

8. What is his or her least favorite school subject?
9. What is his or her favorite subject?
10. What has your child done that he or she feels most proud of?
11. What is his or her biggest complaint about the family?
12. What sport does he or she most enjoy?
13. What is his or her favorite TV program?
14. What really makes him or her angry?
15. What would your child like to be when he or she grows up?
16. What chore does your child like least?
17. What three foods does your child most like?
18. What is your child's most prized possession?
19. What is his or her favorite family occasion?
20. What activity did your child most enjoy last weekend?[4]

The more you are actively there for your child, the more you are apt to know the answers to those questions, I believe.

Of course, the best preventive advice is: *Keep the family together.* In the face of reality, however, we may need help to "be there" after the family has crumbled.

OVERCOMING "BEING THERE" OBSTACLES

Maybe you are facing a personally discouraging situation. A great amount of unattended time has passed. The communication has broken down. Perhaps you've already missed years of your children's lives. You don't think you can reestablish relationship, even though you'd like to. Therefore, let me introduce you to a remarkable man.

Meet Charles Ballard.

As a seventeen-year-old, Charles had fathered a son. Soon afterward, he was sent to prison. His life was in a downward spiral until he met a remarkable fellow-inmate, who spoke to him of God's love. Charles was responsive and accepted Jesus into his life. It was the beginning of many changes that would make a drastic impact upon the direction of Charles's life. The older prisoner spoke to him about taking responsibility for the life he had fathered. He challenged Charles, upon his release, to find his child and become involved in his life. From this older Christian man, Charles was personally discipled in the responsibilities of parenthood.

When he was released, Charles followed through on his convictions. Even though his girlfriend had married another man, he became involved in the care and parenting of the child he had conceived with her. Soon he was preaching the love of God and parental responsibility to other troubled inner-city young men.

In 1982 the National Institute for Responsible Fatherhood and Family Development was founded. Charles Ballard is the president. Since then, more than two thousand young men with backgrounds similar to Charles's have been helped. Each young man is challenged to marry the mother of his child or, if that proves impossible, to improve relationship with her and establish paternity with his child.

The success rate of this approach is evident. Some do marry the mother of their children. An amazing ninety percent establish paternity with their children. Another 96.2 percent report improved relationships with the mother of the children as well as with their children themselves.

Amazing!

What obstacles are in your way of "being there" for your children? Is it as big a gap as prison, or remarriage, or poor relationship? You can mend the break. You can begin to share life with your child.

My personal feeling is that it is almost never too late to learn to connect. Being close to one's parents is the deepest longing of a child's heart, and no matter how old the child becomes, it is a stubborn longing that can't be outgrown.

Chances are your attempts to connect and "be there" will be welcomed by your child. Remember, you don't have to be perfect, but you *do* need *to be present*.

Then little children were brought to Jesus for him to place his hands on them and pray for them . . . Jesus said, "Let the little children come to me, and do not hinder them, for the kingdom of heaven belongs to such as these." When he had placed his hands on them, he went on from there.

MATTHEW 19:13–15

ELEVEN
THE HEALING POWER OF TOUCH:
The Connecting Parent

What is your earliest childhood memory? My first memory is of my father rocking me in a large mission-style rocker. It creaked. My father sang. I even remember the smell of his body, the red mole on his cheek, the calm I felt in his hairy and engulfing arms. I think this experience has stayed with me not only because of the intense closeness of the moment, but also because I remember feeling so adoringly in love with him.

Our parents form our future ability to give, receive, and interpret love. When my father died, I was heartbroken. And even though I was an adult woman with two sons, my husband comforted me by holding me like a little girl, rocking me in a big creaky rocker, and singing soothing songs to me. I will take that memory to the grave—the sensation of being comforted, the luxury of being fragile and protected, yes, but also the overwhelming sense of being, at that moment, so in love with my husband, a man so much like my father!

Being held, being touched is by definition a sensual experience. It is physical, but at the same time, it is so much more than that. Touch bonds us to each other. It is one of the important facets of becoming attached and staying attached with our children.

Our parents form our future ability to give, receive, and interpret love.

RELATIONAL PRINCIPLE #7:
CHILDREN NEED TO STAY IN TOUCH WITH THEIR PARENTS.

Many parents are confused about what is appropriate when it comes to touching their children. In the current climate of child sexual abuse, with so much societal focus on the problem, it might be surprising to realize that some children are experiencing the opposite treatment: Some children are denied touch by their parents. In some circles, this is actually being taught. These children will not be shattered in the way abused children are, but they will be damaged, just the same. What happens to a child when appropriate touch is absent? Well, let me illustrate.

I visited a home recently in which both parents had backgrounds of abuse—physical, emotional, sexual. There were three children in their family. The oldest boy, a kindergartner, was very shy, but he began to warm up, and in no time he was trying to sit beside me at supper, bringing books to me to read to him, cuddling up close as we read. I thought nothing of it. When it was bedtime, he came to the landing several times and smiled at me and said, "Goodnight, Mrs. Bell!"

After the children were in bed, the young mother opened up. "You seem so comfortable with Aaron! He really likes you! But I feel so bad. We're never like that with each other. Maybe because I had so many babies in a row and he was the oldest—always getting shoved off my lap by someone younger."

I tried to assure her that she had a big job with three little ones. She stopped me. "It's not that I don't have time and energy. I'm afraid to touch him."

TOUCH-HUNGRY

How sad! Aaron was touch-hungry. He really wanted physical closeness with his mom, but obviously a substitute would do—a mom-for-a-night, we could say. If you were starving for touch, you might be vulnerable to anyone who initially seemed nice. Pedophiles know that. I

140

gently pointed out to her that her approach was dangerous, that her son could be attracted to anyone who might show him affection.

She agreed with me. She had seen it before her very eyes that evening. To deprive a child of touch is another kind of cruelty. As we talked, I learned that she had not come to her conclusions simply as a reaction to her own background of sexual abuse. She had been taught. An older woman had lectured at their church on the dangers of touch between parents and children of the opposite sex. In this woman's mind, all touch was potentially sexual and therefore dangerous and to be avoided.

Misinformation abounds!

HOW TO DEAL WITH MIXED PARENTAL FEELINGS

It's true that our parental emotions can be a mixed bag. How do we handle this area of physical closeness with our children without becoming sexually conflicted? I defer to an expert at this point. Dr. Ross Campbell, a medical doctor, explains that "(1) Every child, regardless of age, needs appropriate physical contact; (2) to have some occasional sexual feelings or fleeting sexual fantasies regarding a child is normal; (3) a parent should ignore these inappropriate feelings, go ahead, and give a child what he or she needs, including appropriate (non-seductive) physical contact."[1]

BUT MY CHILD DOESN'T LIKE TO BE TOUCHED

Another approach I've heard is the idea that not all children receive love through touch. In other words, if your child holds you at arm's length, pushes your hand off his or her shoulder, and walks a block behind you at all times, don't worry. It just isn't important to that child to be touched. The theory goes that you can just forget about touching that child and move on to other ways of expressing your affection.

This theory must have been hatched when the author was raising pubescent sons! At certain ages, children will fend off physical displays of affection as if they were deathly allergic to them! But it's a phase, a developmental stage that children pass through. It doesn't mean that such a child doesn't need physical affection anymore. If the parent falls for it, and withholds touch, it can be the beginning of disconnecting in an important area. Some teenagers have come into their raging hormonal years touch-hungry, distanced from the physical affection of their parents, vulnerable to any offer that comes along.

What to do? They don't want to be hugged, or kissed, or treated like a baby, right? Do you know why? Because their sexual self is emerging. They are confused about appropriate and inappropriate touch. This is an important time for the parent to hang in there and model affectionate touch that is separate from sexuality.

Our sons at eighteen and fifteen are very affectionate. They will put an arm around me in public, give me a peck in front of their friends, and say, "Love you!" We still hold hands and talk. And while they no longer get into bed with us to cuddle, or sit on my lap to be read to, or enjoy being tickled, our connecting through touch continues.

They've passed through the "embarrassed to be touched" stage. But, while they were in that time of their lives, I didn't let them shove me away. I adjusted my public displays of affection for their sake but still initiated affection at home through the safest, most unthreatening type of parental touch.

CREATIVE AGE-APPROPRIATE WAYS TO STAY IN TOUCH

The type of touch that's appropriate changes through the years. Some form of touch should endure. We need touch rituals in order to stay connected. While other forms of touch affection have been discarded because they are now age-inappropriate, these touch rituals remain.

- The men in the family have a custom of gathering in the family room every night. There the back-massage rite is performed. Each takes his turn lying on the floor while a very ritualized massage is given. Some men have other versions of male-bonding—wrestling, roughhousing, and so on. Even sports, despite its obvious competitive theme, is full of bumping, touching, physical contact. I'm sure it fills the touch gap for many men. Just watch professional athletes. They are so comfortable slamming and hitting each other's bodies. They hug and tousle each other. They even pick each other up just as in that commercial of the man and woman running to each other in the field, culminating in the woman's being swept off her feet by the love of her life. Off the playing field, they would never think of doing that with another man! From an admittedly female perspective, I suspect that football, that most macho of all sports, isn't just about winning and chasing a pigskin ball around toward a goal but about being able to stay connected physically in a way that is accepted by society. Now, before I lose all the male readers, let me hurry to explain—that is perfectly okay! Whether it's wrestling or football or massages, it's all a version of touch that serves the same purpose—staying connected.

- We have a calming ritual that is wonderful for small children who have to sit still in a long church service. I've seen my children calm down from being extremely upset using this technique. It's called an "assagemay" (pig latin for *massage*). This is still a requested technique at our home! It's basically a hand massage. We start with the palm and back of their hand, pressing for several minutes between our fingers, in a gentle pinch. Each finger is given the same treatment. Then, as if their fingers are the scaffolding of a small roller coaster, we lightly run a finger up and down between the fingers, across the webbing as the finale. Be careful if you start this. It's proven addictive at our house!

- Any care of the body can be done with a nurturing touch. Before the day of portable hair dryers, my grandmother would towel-dry our hair until it was practically dry, which amounted to a wonderful head massage. Think about the ways you touch your child while you are washing, combing, brushing, styling, manicuring them. All these functions can be performed with a gentle touch that makes such experiences real stress-busters. Look at the adult world and what we're willing to pay for a professional manicure, pedicure, facial, massage, or hairstyle. I recently had my hair washed by a shampooist who was so wonderful—the water temperature was perfect, her fingers applying just the right pressure, no water down my back—that I went back to the salon for her, not necessarily the hair stylist!

- When we say the blessing at mealtime, we make a family ritual of holding hands. It's a small gesture, but one which may keep you connecting during those "Please don't touch me" years!

An aside to parents of infants: With babies it's important that they be held as much as possible when nursing either at breast or from a bottle. It does little good to go through the considerable effort of breast-feeding if a mother props her baby at her breast and uses her hands to do other things during that time. The idea is to use the time to connect and relax from other activities! I know it's not always convenient, but as much as possible, resist the urge to prop up bottles or breasts and move into the next more interesting activity!

The ways to be affectionate and stay connected through touch are more than simply kissing and hugging! Nurturing parents will stand a good chance of staying close with their children if they develop a repertoire of touch that can travel well into the family's later years.

Steve and I went out to breakfast one Saturday recently. We had to wait, so we sat down and watched people. We were both attracted to an extended family that was gathering and waiting in the lobby in front of us. It consisted of an older grandmother (quite elderly but well-groomed, dressed sportily, the kind of woman who makes you realize there is life after age seventy-five!), the parents, and their adult married children and grandchildren. As each group arrived, they were affectionately greeted with hugs and kisses. Grandma kissed everyone. Everyone kissed each other. Everyone got hugged and kissed about fifteen times that morning. What a great start to the day! No one had come from far away. This was obviously their normal way of welcoming one another. The sense of belonging was clear.

How nice! I must remember that as our boys marry and others come into the family!

I stood in line at the grocery store behind a woman and her aging mother. To pass the time, the middle-aged daughter gently massaged her mother's shoulders and neck. It was done matter-of-factly. At one point the mother said, "Oh, that feels so good, but, I should be doing this for you!" Her daughter replied, "You have, Mom. It's your turn now!"

How wonderful! They had never stopped touching. They were still able to connect with each other through something as simple as a touch to the neck or shoulder.

But, what if you're not a touchy-feely type? What will happen if you don't stay touch-connected with your children?

Your children will survive if you don't express your feelings—but we're not speaking of survival. We're talking about attachment—the spiritual and emotional aspects of parenting. To be close, you will need to develop a level of comfort with expressing affection physically.

It's interesting and sad to note that in India the lowest class in the Hindu caste system is called "the untouchables." Their position in society carries the stigma of being loathsome and repulsive.

To be "untouchable" carries a deep emotional message of rejection.

In contrast to that attitude, it's interesting that the healing miracles of Jesus often involved touch. The gospels record, time and again, incidents such as:

- A woman with fever was visited by Jesus. He took her hand and helped her up. *She was immediately healed* to the extent that she was able to wait on Jesus and his disciples.
- Seeing a leper, Jesus was filled with compassion. He reached out to the man and touched him. *Immediately the man was cured.*
- A little girl had died. Jesus came to her and took her by the hand. "Little girl, get up!" he commands. *Immediately she stood up and walked around.*
- After he took him aside, away from the crowd, Jesus put his fingers into the man's ears. Then he spit and touched the man's tongue. He looked up to heaven and with a deep sigh said to him, "Be opened!" *At this, the man could hear and speak plainly.*
- Some people brought a blind man and begged Jesus to touch him. He took the blind man by the hand and led him outside the village. He then spit on the man's eyes and put his hands on him. When Jesus asked, "Do you see anything?" He looked up and said, "I see people; they look like trees walking around." Once more Jesus put his hands on the man's eyes. Then he saw everything clearly.
- *And as many as touched him were made whole.*

In many instances, Jesus healed without touching, sometimes without even seeing the person being healed. Was touching a part of the modus operandi for miracles, or was it something else? Did it heal the part of the sick person that felt unclean, unlovable, and rejected? Was it a gesture of identification and compassionate connecting?

We can only wonder. Yet, it is meticulously recorded time after time. *And he touched . . . and he put his hands upon him.*

Touch. Whether from the hand of Jesus or from the hand of a parent, its healing, connecting properties are wonderful! Touch.

Whether it's the memory of being rocked and sung to as a little girl, or of high-fiving it with your dad through your teen years, touch keeps us close. Touch heals the part of us that feels rejection and uncleanliness and unworthiness.

Touch is a gift from God.

Frog and Toad went on a long walk. Toad took the list from his pocket again. He crossed out: Take walk with Frog. Just then there was a strong wind. It blew the list out of Toad's hand. "Help!" cried Toad. "My list is blowing away. What will I do without my list?" "Hurry!" said Frog. "We will run and catch it." "No!" shouted Toad. "Why not?" asked Frog. "Because," wailed Toad, "running after my list is not one of the things that I wrote on my list of things to do!"

ARNOLD LOBEL
Frog and Toad Together

TWELVE
ENCOURAGEMENT FOR THE ORGANIZATIONALLY CHALLENGED:
The Ordered Parent

When it comes to being on top of the details of your children's lives, one of my most shame-filled parental moments happened when our second son, Justin, was in the fifth grade. He had been lobbying for a new pair of expensive gym shoes. Repeatedly he told us that his old pair of shoes was falling apart and that they hurt his feet. His "old" pair of shoes had been purchased only two months before. They hardly looked worn. A little scurfy, maybe, but any parent could see they had miles to go before a trade-in. Now I must tell you, in my weak defense, that this child is extremely persistent and can really ding away at a point when he has his mind set on something.

One night at supper in a display of extreme bad manners, he actually took off his shoe and put his bare foot up on the table.

"Look at what these shoes are doing to my foot, Mom. I really need new ones, bad!"

That did it! He had dinged that bell one too many times for me. Without looking, I ordered him to get his foot off the table, that I was unimpressed, and furthermore, I had no money. He might as well try to get blood out of a turnip!

The next day at school all the parents were invited to attend Greek plays written and presented by the fifth-grade English department. Justin had a lead role as Dionysius. There he was, up on the stage, wrapped in a white sheet, performing beautifully. But my pride soon melted. What was wrong with him? He was limping noticeably. Then I saw it—at parental eye level a blazing, infected ingrown toenail screamed, "Will somebody please take care of me?"

I felt as though someone had put a knife in my heart and was twisting it! I couldn't take my eyes off that amazing toe. Neon-sign-like, it flashed: BAD MOTHER, NEGLECTED CHILD, BAD MOTHER NEGLECTED CHILD. Back and forth on the stage directly under my eye and in view of the entire parental audience, the incriminating toe paraded. How had I missed it?

It seemed like a very long play. As soon as the play was over, I told the teacher I was taking Justin to the doctor *immediately*. She agreed.

When we saw the doctor that afternoon, he said, "Well, you know, Valerie, this toe didn't get like this overnight!"

Guilt!

We learned a great deal that day. I learned that I needed to pay closer attention to the physical details of my children's lives. Justin learned something, too. He learned that you *can* get blood out of a turnip, particularly if the turnip feels guilty. Before the day was over, he was the proud owner of a new pair of gym shoes! I'm sure the new shoes took some of the sting out of the situation, but I also know that Justin's confidence in his parents to meet his needs was eroded somewhat as well.

PARENTAL DISORDER CAUSES KIDS TO SUFFER

When we are disordered, our children suffer. Attention to the details of their lives is an important aspect to feeling well-cared-for.

When the details are in place, a child can relax and have confidence that his or her parents are looking out for his or her well-being. There is a connected feeling between well-cared-for children and their parents.

When we are disordered, our children suffer.

So, although I admit this is not my natural operating style, I also understand that children need the security that comes from a parent who can manage the details of life fairly smoothly. Disorganization is stressful for everyone, but children are unique in that they are dependent on their parents to protect them from the consequences of chaos. When we parents don't follow through as we should, too often our children suffer. When the forms from school aren't filled out, the kids are the ones the teachers scold. When the sports physicals aren't in on time, it's the children who have to deal with coaches who bench them. When piano lessons are forgotten or dental appointments overlooked, too often the kids are the ones who hear about it from the frustrated adult in charge.

But whom does the child resent in such a scenario? You've got it! The parent!

RELATIONAL PRINCIPLE #8:
CHILDREN NEED PARENTS WHO ARE ORDERED.

A Childhood Envy

In my own childhood I only remember envying one other child. My feelings about her didn't have their root in her prettiness, or her intelligence, or her popularity, although she was all those things. I envied her because I thought she was extremely well cared-for. The details of her life were well-tended. She always had rides to after-school activities and never had to wait afterward, wondering if she would be remembered. Her mother was always waiting.

Her clothes were pressed. She had an air of appropriateness about her—from her saddle shoes to her lunch box—everything was clean, polished, and right. I stayed at her house overnight one time but couldn't bear to go back or extend an invitation to my home. The differences were painfully apparent. She had a quilted robe with matching slippers. I didn't know such things existed. She had a bedroom with a canopy bed. For years, I had no assigned place. I would sleep with my sister in her room, or on a couch, wherever there was a space.

At school, her forms were always turned in on time—her name never appeared on the blackboard for truancy. At the appropriate time, her teeth were braced, her hair cut fashionably, she even had a training bra while the rest of us were still wearing underwear.

Her life was ordered! Her life, at least on the physical level, was secure.

My parents had some wonderful qualities, but order was not one of them!

So, I have not been able to rely on the automatic, intrinsic, modeled-from-my-own-childhood approach to this part of life. I have had to learn. And all the while that I acknowledge how important it is for my children, I still have to WORK to even come close to the ideal. Maybe some of you are struggling to discipline yourself to some other parental goal that is not easy for you. Well, I understand completely!

How do you know if you need to become a more ordered parent? You probably don't need a symptom list to identify yourself, but here it is, in case anyone is wondering.

SYMPTOMS OF AN ORGANIZATIONALLY CHALLENGED HOME

- Your children's clothes get washed and dried but sometimes don't make it into their drawers and closets. Your kids rummage for unfolded clean clothes in "after" baskets that look an awful lot like "before" baskets minus the odor.
- The school nurse has your phone number memorized and is threatening to expel your child from school unless you produce an official immunization record.
- The receptionist at the dentist barely manages a hello when you actually remember an appointment, and she is probably lobbying for her boss to drop your family as patients.
- Your child's report card is held because you failed to send in the user's fee for an extracurricular activity.
- You thought the school held back your child's report card, but then weeks later you found it behind the flour canister in the pantry—right where you left it!

- Your doctor said your child's wart is the biggest he's ever seen. What you heard said was, "You negligent parent, why didn't you bring this kid in sooner?"
- The library is threatening to "sue" you for unreturned books.
- Someone got food poisoning from eating out of your refrigerator. Well, you weren't sure, but the turkey sandwich tasted pretty bad, and they chose to take ipecac instead of waiting around for nature to take her course.
- You forgot to call in your child's illness to the attendance office. The school secretary telephones your home and your child answers. He is groggy and says he doesn't know where Mom and Dad are. School officials panic and call your neighbors to see if your child has been abandoned. Your neighbors enjoy telling you about it later . . . again and again and again!
- Your child typically has to borrow lunch money from other kids until tomorrow when you can get to the bank for some cash.

Can you relate? I wish I were inventing everything on that list—but, although I'm embarrassed to admit it, all of these things and more have actually happened at our house!

As an expert at disorganization, I can assure you that this is a very stressful way to live.

WHEN "HINTS FROM HELOISE" DON'T MOVE YOU

The problem is that most things you read and hear concerning organization are written by people who have gone over the system's edge. I will never relate to ideas like alphabetizing your spice drawer or card-cataloging your canned goods. Thanks, but no thanks, I'm not interested in owning my own work apron complete with pockets for sponges, cleaners, and squeegees. I will never buy cleaning products in industrial quantities or learn to wipe surfaces with both hands so I can cut my work time in half. Sorry. That's just not me. I'm repulsed by the possibility of becoming Toad-like, enslaved to a list or hyperorganizational system.

After struggling with this area for years, I've discovered that I need two things: a reasonable system and the discipline to stick to it. And although I know I will resist any approach that's too overwhelming and engulfing, I also know that I need a plan.

So here is my system. Try not to laugh too hard, Heloise! It works for organizationally challenged people like me.

SUGGESTIONS FOR ORDERING YOUR FAMILY LIFE

1. **KEEP A FAMILY MASTER CALENDAR.**
   Logical enough, right? Here's the tricky part—don't forget to consult it! During your family years try to give your kids' agendas top priority. Protect your family times together.

2. **EVERY FAMILY MEMBER HAS AN EQUIPPED WORK SPACE.**
   If *everyone* is equipped, you will be missing your own things less often. Every workspace should include scissors, stationery and stamps, pens, pencils, sharpener, paper, Scotch tape, and so forth.

3. **KEEP FILES.**
   Teach everyone in the family to file the things that will be needed or wanted in the future. This is a must!

4. **KEEP A LIST OF MOST-USED NUMBERS POSTED NEAR PHONES.**
   This will save you the frustration of repeatedly looking up the numbers of your children's friends, the school attendance office, and the piano teacher.

5. **READ MAGAZINES AND NEWSPAPERS, WITH SCISSORS AND FILE AT HAND.**
   I've developed a ritual for my morning reading time. I clip interesting articles to share with my family later or to file away as I'm reading. That way I don't have to search through old piles of newspapers later when I want to remember what was written. I often share these pieces with my family at night. I've found this is a great way to stay informed and connected with each other's ideas.

6. **FOLLOW THROUGH ON ANY PHYSICAL COMPLAINT WITH PROPER MEDICAL ATTENTION.**
   Don't make your kids have to remind you about things that are bothering them physically. Prompt follow-through on requests translates into a sense of being well-cared for.

7. **FILL OUT SCHOOL FORMS WHEN YOU RECEIVE THEM.**
   Be the first family to return school paperwork. Get it out of your hair and returned to the proper people as soon as possible.

8. REGULARLY EDIT YOUR PHYSICAL SPACE.

   Give away outgrown or unused clothing. Everything you own must be taken care of. So don't keep things you don't care about. Give away books that aren't "keepers." Simplify.

9. KEEP SURFACES CLEAR OF CLUTTER.

   Have a place for magazines, another for catalogs. Store day-old papers out of sight until ready to be recycled. Create a place for all the paper that comes into your house. Declutter bathroom counters before you leave the room. Don't let piles accumulate.

10. GET HELP!

    You don't need to hire expensive professional help. Recruit neighbor children. Ask a friend for help and then return the favor. Don't wait until you go under organizationally. When necessary (and for some of us it's almost always necessary), get help to stay on top of the cleaning and other household organizational chores.

Helping your child organize the mountains of informational paper, homework, permission slips, junk mail, and so forth that pass through your home in his or her lifetime is a great service. Clean sheets, organized rooms, a personal space, clothes hanging ready to wear in the closet . . . all of these give a child a well-cared-for feeling.

And remember, provide this care without resentment or a sense of drudgery that communicates, "Taking care of you is a drag!" Every time the papers go back to school signed on time, every time the medical forms are completed before school begins in the fall, every time you help your child be on top of the details of his or her life, you communicate "I love you," and in so doing, provide your child with a great sense of security.

Be proactive. Initiate replacing worn-out shoes. Be aware enough to know when notebooks need replacement or clothes are getting too small. Don't be passive and reactive.

For the parent who's tuned in, there's an opportunity in every responsibility—another chance to demonstrate the care and love you feel for your child.

Why do we love home-cooked meals? Because someone has gone to the trouble of showing us through their efforts that we matter to them. Why does a laundry room smell so appealing? Because the smell of soap and softener communicates the care someone is providing us. Why are handmade gifts so treasured? Because the organization, creativity, and care involved in such a gift all communicate that secure sense of belonging to someone who loves us in special ways.

For the parent who's tuned in, there's an opportunity in every responsibility—another chance to demonstrate the care and love you feel for your child.

The good news is that we parents don't need to be intimidated by the organizational gurus. We don't need to be slaves to our systems, but we *do* need to pay close enough attention to the details of our children's lives so they know that they matter.

*In the desert the whole community grumbled against Moses
and Aaron. The Israelites said to them, "If only we had died
by the Lord's hand in Egypt! There we sat around pots of
meat and ate all the food we wanted, but you have brought
us out into this desert to starve this entire assembly to death!"*

EXODUS 16:2, 3

THIRTEEN
WHEN GOING BACK TO EGYPT SEEMS APPEALING

When I hear the phrases, the wording, the questions we ask as
a parenting culture, I realize that many of us are attracted to a parenting
style that takes the path of least resistance. Books with titles like, *Good
Enough Parenting*, questions like, "How much time can I leave my child
home alone during the week?"—phrases like "quality time"— all lower
the role of parent to that of damage controller. In other words, I hear our
culture asking in many different ways, "How little can I give to this child-
raising project without having a negative impact on my child?"

Many parents, like me, are not going to be satisfied with parenting on that minimal-effort level. I want to be the best parent I can be.
I don't want to just limit the potential damage—my husband and I want
to be one of our children's greatest assets.

If you're like me, you want to find out the answers to another
whole set of questions that we're not hearing asked in our culture at
large. Don't talk to us about "good enough," tell us how to *excel* at this
important job of parenting. Don't tell me that most kids "survive" lonely
childhoods without available parents. Don't pacify me and tell me what
you think I want to hear. Tell me the truth. Don't throw me a glossy

women's-magazine line! These are my kids—what I hold dearest in my life. Don't appease and placate me when their well-being is at stake!

Approaches to parenting that are meant to alleviate guilt will be unsatisfying to a highly motivated parent. We want relationship with our children . . . not simply toleration. We want attachment . . . not just shared living space. We care deeply. Amazingly, we strive and sacrifice to give our children the emotional gifts and spiritual helps we never even received ourselves. Even more amazingly, we often succeed!

We parents who care more than we're encouraged to care, who give because we can't imagine withholding, who dedicate our family years to meeting our children's needs, are a courageous, counterculture group.

For such a parent, all that I've shared has been a primer, review material for a course in Parenting 101. I hope, if you are such a parent, that you will feel reassured—and confident. I trust you've felt as you read that you were looking in a mirror at your own parenting style.

GOOD-PARENT RECOGNITION

Recently, I met such a mom after a seminar I gave on parenting. I was seated in the front pew, trying to give my feet a rest after a long day of teaching. She knelt in front of me. *Here's a mom who knows the importance of eyeball to eyeball communication*, I thought. In a whisper, as if she were confiding a great secret she said, "I'm so glad to hear your approach to parenting. That's how we do it at our house. Our family is close. Our kids have never been a problem. They're excelling in school. But, until I heard you today, I never felt affirmed. I've felt like I was swimming against the usual tides of parental advice. What a relief!"

Wouldn't it be wonderful if we could hand out awards or some kind of public recognition for people who are excelling in the crucial and difficult job of parenting? Wouldn't a parental variation on the "Good Housekeeping Seal of Approval" be kind of neat? You know, something shiny and big that would fit on your fridge where everyone couldn't help but see it? Or how about a pink car with a bumper sticker that proclaimed, "This Driver Is the Parent of the Year!" How about a television talk show that interviews healthy families about the healthy impact their parents bestowed? Would you cheer for a Great Parent Parade? How about special pins awarded to recognize parents who never missed their kids' ball games, or who drove their car packed with kids to every event? Wouldn't it be awesome to be affirmed in your role of parent?

If you feel you are on track, then let me say to you, "Good. Good for you!" If you feel you have a reason for parental confidence, then relax a little and enjoy these family years to the max. You're on the right track!

Another group of parents are feeling overwhelmed by the responsibilities of everyday child care.

THE APPEAL OF EGYPT AND THE STRUGGLE TO CHANGE

I spoke with such a woman recently after a church meeting. She represents the typical 1990s parental conundrum. Educated, successful in her career, at ease socially, she looks together. But as we talked and the conversation moved toward children, another woman emerged.

"Why doesn't anyone tell me how to be a parent?" she asked. "Why didn't my mother teach me anything? Who has the answers, and why aren't they talking about it?"

The mother side of this woman was frustrated, feeling incompetent, and maybe even a little angry.

Part of this woman's dilemma is that no one has all the answers. I know that I don't, but I am motivated to share what I do know because my heart goes out to people who are frustrated with their parental role. My hope is to help unfocused and confused parents. I want to help them have a clear direction, an achievable goal, a framework on which to build a healthy family system, a reason for confidence.

Interestingly, I had just spent an hour speaking to this woman about the things I've learned about parenting. They had as much impact on her as water has on a duck's back.

I had given her answers. I had talked about it. Why hadn't she been able to hear me?

Because she resisted such a radical change from her natural methods.

She was suffering from the "I want to go back to Egypt" syndrome. I'm referring to the interesting human tendency to stay with the familiar; even though it may be heartbreaking and abusive, there is still the comfort of staying with what is known. Scripture gives us a glimpse into this facet of human nature in the story of the children of Israel and their deliverance from Egypt by Moses. Slavery was heartbreaking. Then God delivered them, and when they watched their enemies go down into the waves, they danced and sang songs of deliverance on the dry sea banks. But they were not prepared for the hardships of the desert wandering and, in time, they forgot the difficulties of life in slavery and resisted the hard work of achieving a better life.

Changing parenting styles can be hard work that makes going back to the conditions in Egypt seem more appealing than doing the intentional work of becoming a relational nurturing parent!

In fact, my sense is that many parents, after reading the previous chapters, are drawn back to Egypt. Let me explain. What is Egypt? It's the instinctive parenting style you could do without thinking much about it. In Egypt you could achieve the image of being a good parent, go through the good-parent motions, without bothering to really connect with your kids, and no one is the wiser. In Egypt you could be controlling and overbearing, and numerous people applauded you for disciplining your kids and making them stay in line.

Maybe your own parents lived in Egypt and, as far as you can see, you turned out okay. In Egypt you focused on what your kids were doing wrong, not on yourself, and that's much more comfortable, right?

Good ol' Egypt—where you had plenty of company for your rocky parental journey.

Let me say this, "Don't go back to Egypt!"

Choosing to live in Egypt when you have a map to a better place is foolish. Choosing to live in Egypt because it's familiar and comfortable is understandable, but it's wimping out!

Go back to Egypt? It's a sure way to kill the dreams you hold for close relationship with your children.

Go back to Egypt? I can promise you'll never become the person or parent God intended you to be.

Go back to Egypt? It's almost a certainty that you'll break your children's hearts.

My Own Temptation Toward Egypt

Let me encourage you with some personal observations. At every crucial developmental stage of my life I have felt the almost irresistible pull of going back to some kind of Egypt. For instance, a recent parenting Egypt for me involved holding back on the advice and allowing the boys as they've gotten older to make their own decisions more often (including sometimes making mistakes) without imposing my choices. I know they need to sense that I have confidence in their perceptions and choices. My natural instinct is to offer advice, protect them from consequences, before I've been invited to share my opinion.

But I'm learning. I'm making fewer unsolicited judgments and I'm listening more. I recognize the pattern that accompanies my relationally destructive tendency. It's the allure of good old comfortable Egypt. But every time I've gathered my courage and ignored the interior voices that suggested I couldn't handle the change, I made great personal strides. It takes great courage to continue to grow! We can experience strong interior resistance to personal change.

But you know what? You don't have to go back to Egypt. You can achieve the family life you want. You were meant for a better place, a healthier life, even a piece of the Garden of Eden. Go for it!

There is so much at stake. It is crucial that we parents are attachable and that we connect with our children. I believe the societal evidence is pointing to the fact that our children are vulnerable to developmental problems if they don't receive the protection of emotional connection with their parents.

WHAT'S AT RISK

A child who is convinced that he or she is unlovable, because he or she has been unable to bond with a parent, may develop a group of symptoms that read like something out of a tale of family horror. As I share the following list with parents, there is always a strong response. Many parents have acknowledged to me that their child has these symptoms, that they have sought out traditional therapy, and no one has been able to identify the problem. One man who is principal of an alternative high school for troubled teenagers told me that this list describes every kid in his high school!

If you're thinking about going back to Egypt, take a look at these troubling characteristics to which detached children seem to be prone. Think again before you take the path of least resistance.

SYMPTOMS OF CHARACTER-DISTURBED CHILDREN

1. Lack of ability to give and receive affection
2. Self-destructive behavior
3. Cruelty to others or to pets
4. Phoniness
5. Stealing, hoarding, and gorging
6. Lack of long-term childhood friends

7. Extreme control problems
8. Speech pathology
9. Abnormalities in eye contact
10. The parents seem unreasonably angry
11. Preoccupation with blood, fire, and gore
12. Superficial attractiveness and friendliness with strangers
13. Learning disorders
14. Crazy lying[1]

Does it seem like a strange combination of traits? The common factor behind each symptom is the child's belief that he or she is unlovable. It's as if the child's interior voice says, *If I can drive adults crazy, it affirms that I am unlovable and makes me feel as if I were the one in control with my crazy-making.*

You can see that such characteristics would lead to major trouble in a child's future life. To me, it explains so much of the antisocial behavior that seems to be rampant in parts of the adolescent community today.

And what is the chief cause of the breakdown of such children? Many in the child-development field believe it is caused by lack of bonding, an emotionally detached relationship between a child and his or her parents.

I don't know about you, but that always sends a chill up my parental spine!

How we parent is crucial. Egypt is really not an acceptable alternative for such troubled family times.

FOLLOW YOUR HEART

I am firmly convinced that in homes where "something is missing" the emotional gap can be filled with relationship. I restate my conviction that parenting is a skill that *can* be learned, once you know what's involved.

And what about all the difficult situations that come up in a day of parenting? What about the times when you wonder what in the world to do? Look to your heart. If you love your child, your heart already knows the way. Be confident. You know your part. Play it well.

PARENTING: THE GREATEST SELF-DISCIPLINE

Our youngest son is a football player. Every fall the players and parents gather at the beginning of the season for a motivational talk. We are assured that our sons' involvement in football will make a positive difference in their development. During the sessions, the coaches often wax on about the great disciplines our sons will learn under their tutelage. That may be true, but every time I hear that speech I want to stand up and put it all in perspective. I want to say something like, "Well, that may be true, but just wait until they become *parents*! Then they'll really learn about self-discipline! Football, piano lessons, homework, are all child's play compared to the discipline of parenting!"

I have spared my son that public embarrassment. After all, it's the coach's party, not mine. But, it's true, isn't it? There's no discipline like parenting for the development of the inner person. Nothing is so day to day, moment to moment. There are no breaks in the parenting schedule, no vacations from it, no national holidays to get away from it. It's constant!

Parenting is the great life equalizer.

What else requires patience and graciousness in the middle of some sleep-robbed night? Where else can you learn the servant spirit required in the cleaning up after a round of child-puking? What other area of life stretches us in humility like nursing a baby, with the months of soaked underwear and rounds of dressing, only to turn around half an hour later to undress again? What else can make us so vulnerable, teach us about handling fear and anxiety, than a child who is hurting and struggling? Is there anything as effective in tenderizing us? Is there anything more equalizing in life than sitting with other parents who all smell of peanut butter and jelly, who may realize for the first time in life that they don't have all the answers?

Parenting is the great life equalizer. We are all humbled by the experience.

What grows up our inner child more than becoming a parent? Can you see that it's part of a great design? I view it as a divine plan to accelerate our own growth. It's a doubled-edged sword that accomplishes two purposes: the protection and formation of the child and the maturation of the parent.

You know it kind of smacks of divine genius! God's fingerprints are all over the crazy but wonderful blueprint.

161

THE TRUTH OF WHAT THE OLD WOMEN SAY

I am nearing the end of my child-raising years. I have become like all the older women who told me that these years would go fast. Many of them tried to warn me. I guess I really didn't believe them. Honestly, it's hard to comprehend the concept of "fast" when a day with a two-year-old can seem like an eternity. I probably thought it was just a cliché, something that older women were required to say to young mothers, but they were right. If anything, it was understated.

Turn around—your baby is walking.

Turn again, and your child is in love with the kindergarten teacher.

Blink, and it's time for sleepovers and Little League.

Soon—too soon—you hand your car keys to a son either to pick up a corsage, or to a daughter on her way to college. Not long ago, I sat with my firstborn son, Brendan, the night before he was a freshman, college bound. I was experiencing some inner turmoil. I was excited for him. I was certain he'd love college. But I found myself wondering if we had told him all that he needed for life. He was leaving. Had we left huge gaps? I wondered if we were sufficiently attached so that he would occasionally want to come home again.

It's hard to hold on to someone who's sprouting wings. The time had come. My "Samuel" had an appointment with his heavenly Parent—it was time to let him go into his spiritual Father's tutelage.

The involvement of God as a heavenly Parent in our children's lives is the thought I comfort myself with. I do not parent alone. Nor do you. We have a divine partner in the parenting venture. He can fill the gaps of which we're unaware. He covers our mistakes, compensates for our inadequacies. He is the child's true parent. Our children never truly "belong" to us anyway. We are temporary caretakers, just human witnesses to the wonders of birth and the miracle of life and the development of love.

It's an awesome responsibility and trust we've been given.

A FOND FAREWELL

This book is nearly ended. It's odd, but I find myself feeling some of the same feelings about this written child that I did about Brendan as he left for college. Have I left big gaps? Have I been as helpful as you need me to be? With mixed feelings I realize that this, my "mind child," is leaving me and going into another life where it will be edited, published, critiqued, well- or poorly received, or perhaps even ignored. Whatever lies ahead for this child, I realize that soon my words will be in stone, not just a part of my creative process. I will have been committed to them and identified with them from now on. Maybe this is "finisher's remorse."

But perhaps it's something else. You see, in the months I've spent writing, I have had a special relationship with you. You have been so much in my mind. You are what has motivated me. I have seen the tears, the frustration, and been moved. Every day I have kept that image of you in front of me.

To you, parent! May you be your family's greatest asset.

So I leave you with compassion for your struggles to be the parent your child needs you to be. My strong conviction is that you can excel.

I leave you with anticipation of the person you are becoming. You are growing. This is as awe-inspiring, to me, as amazing as watching any one-year-old learn to walk. You have the potential to be a better parent this year than you were before. Exciting!

In a strange way, I will miss the awareness of you in my daily life. In the process of writing for you, I have found myself on your side. I hope you know that I am for you!

It's hard to let go of this child and say goodbye, but it, too, is sprouting wings. It will have a life of its own every time it is read. And I am comforted that God will cover my inadequacy. I must trust him to help you interpret and apply whatever truth is needed in your life. So I leave you with a variation of the goodbye with which my youngest son graces most mornings of my life: "Love you, Mama. Have a great day!"

It's not only a farewell. It's a blessing as well.

To you, parent! May you be your family's greatest asset. May your children rise up and called you blessed. May you experience the intimacy and closeness you long for with your children. Parent with confidence. Parent with delight. Enjoy your family years. I have given you the "secrets" that have helped me during my own family years. Now all I have left to give is my farewell. My love, parent. Have a great family!

Woe to that land that's governed by a child!

SHAKESPEARE

APPENDIX
Questions Parents Ask

As I've had opportunity to share my ideas with parent groups, I've usually ended the sessions with a question-and-answer time. Most of the questions tend to recycle from group to group. They're hard, but they are also excellent questions in light of the material that's been presented. So here are a few of the most-asked questions. Hopefully, something that you might be wondering about will be covered by some of these questions about the loose ends of parent-child relationships.

1. Can't you spoil a child if you meet all of his or her needs?

First, let me assure you that no parents, anywhere, at any time, no matter how dedicated, have ever managed to meet all of their child's needs. So be assured that meeting your child's needs is not the formula for producing a brat.

We would have no brats if we met all our child's needs.

But, you also know that obnoxious, self-centered children abound. How do you raise a brat? Brats are often children who have become powerful because Mom and Dad have met all their inappropriate needs and demands and have surrendered to emotional extortion. Simply put—brats are kids who can run all over their parents.

Insecure parents who lack confidence in their ability to parent, who are afraid to discipline for fear of losing their child's love, who fail to follow through with consequences when their child has behaved inappropriately, often create their own home-grown brats.

Without realizing it, these parents are often subconsciously asking the question, "What do I need?" One brat I watched grow up could really throw a fit. She refused to eat anything her mother, who was a fine cook, served. She became powerful at mealtimes through fits, refusal to eat, and generally bratty behavior. If the parents had asked, "What does this child need?" the right answer would have been, "To eat what's put before her." Hunger is a great teacher of such a lesson. Instead they asked, "How can we get this kid to shut up?" Every night became a trip to a fast-food restaurant to appease this powerful mite of an emotional extortionist. ANYTHING for peace! They did that child no favors—she became a very unlikable child, a powerful child, a brat.

What that child really needed was parents who defined the boundaries of behavior and made sure that she complied with the standards set. A child needs the security of living with parents who are helping them to learn to live well—and that means within certain acceptable boundaries.

If parents will ask the primary parenting question, "What does this child need?" they will often find that the answer is *discipline*—and *now*. Never allow your child to become powerful through refusing to obey, humiliating you through public scenes, or private emotional resistance meant to wear down your resolve. Never get into the bad habit of arguing your point with a child. WALK AWAY if you need to—but don't stand there and argue your point. Let your child know that such behavior will get him or her in deep weeds! Don't tolerate it! If you said it and it wasn't done, if you said it and they balked by arguing about it— THAT'S DISOBEDIENCE—the argumentative spirit is as much a problem as the incomplete instructions.

Amazingly, some parents are unsure of what the rest of the world knows without a doubt. Is your child a brat? Is he or she spoiled rotten? What kind of feedback do people give you about your child? If others tell you that your child is a brat, he or she probably is! It doesn't matter if *you* can tolerate your child's behavior, the child needs your help to avoid turning off everyone else! My advice would be, make sure your child knows who the parent is—NOW! Eventually your child will need to fit into the social structure of this world, which will be impossible if the child thinks he always has to have his way.

We often said to our boys, "You are just along for the ride. You are not a voting member in this particular decision-making process. This is not a democracy but a parentocracy! *We* will decide, not you!" If it sounds mean to you, let me assure you it was a concept that kept us out of McDonald's every night, that helped us take vacations that restored us, and gave us some space from the outrageous demands of childishness.

Remember, a brat is a child whose parents have met all his or her inappropriate needs and wants, who has worn out his or her parents through emotional intimidation—not a child whose real needs have been consistently met by Mom and Dad.

2. My child thinks he needs the most expensive athletic shoes, the latest stereo components, the latest styles in clothing. We can't afford this kid! What should we do?

If you ask, "What does this child really need?" you might come up with the answer, "To learn the value of the dollar," or "To learn to discern between real need and wants or desires." We are obligated as parents to meet our children's needs. Be that as it may, I am so glad my parents understood and now my husband understands that it sometimes breaks my heart if my desires beyond food and shelter aren't met. Part of any close relationship is understanding the other person's hot buttons. If your child is dying for a pair of one-hundred-dollar shoes and you think fifty dollars is the max your wallet and conscience can go, then you might try this—give him or her the fifty dollars and let hard work earn the rest. Thus, everyone wins. The child learns how much work goes into that amount of money. You have taught your values. No one is angry or hurt.

3. What about spanking?

I guess I must say that we believe in it, because our children have been spanked. In the face of obstinate defiance or total disrespect, we have occasionally spanked our boys, but through the years I have developed a growing distaste for it as a regular approach to discipline. My negative feelings about spankings go beyond my own taste, however. More and more I'm convinced that it can be very dangerous. Just as marijuana is considered the gateway drug to more addictive drugs, the first drug that leads to other more dangerous ones, I see spanking as having the potential to be the gateway to physical child abuse. In a society that has problems with parents killing their own children, I have a hard time recommending spanking as a usual disciplinary method. I particularly see spanking as dangerous when it is used not as the last parental straw but rather as the disciplinary starting point. If you regularly start with spanking, what could possibly follow but more heavy physical discipline that is most probably abusive?

During the year 1993, the *Chicago Tribune* ran front-page articles every time a child was killed in the city. The fifty-fifth child, a twenty-one-month old, was disciplined and killed for playing with food in the refrigerator. Speaking of how discipline can lead to death at the hands of parents, one article said, "These were their [the dead children's] crimes: Playing with food in the refrigerator. Splashing water in the toilet. Touching the television set. Wetting the bed. Talking back. Crying.

Their punishment was death. People who know little about child development and have unrealistic expectations of children's capabilities are more likely to be abusive toward them."[1]

Permission to use physical punishment combined with lack of parental control and ignorance of child development is too often a deadly combination.

But what about the Scripture that says, "Spare the rod and spoil the child"? I believe the principle is true. But, I see this Scripture as defining principle, not necessarily prescribing method. I say again and again: Be sure there are consequences for misbehavior.

Our boys have rarely been spanked, and then, mostly before the grade school years. My sense is that there is something wrong in a family where a child is regularly physically disciplined. More and more this is questionable in our society and regarded as child abuse.

> In a home where relationship and trust abound, physical punishment is rarely necessary.

Children respond to spanking in one of two ways—either they are shattered by it and the trust between the parent and child is endangered, or they become callous and it has little impact.

Spanking creates an atmosphere of fear, intimidation, and domination. If you must use it, be careful, and whatever you do, *be in control.* The attached parent-child couple will have little need for such extreme methods of problem solving. In a home where relationship and trust abound, physical punishment is rarely necessary. Thank heavens!

Christian leaders who advocate spanking must be willing to accept responsibility for the horrific way this is translated into children's lives. I am not willing to give ground to certain parents who think they have the right to beat their children to pulp. They can never say, "But, Valerie Bell said . . ." I must follow my conscience in this delicate matter.

My inner spirit says: Parents, find a kinder, gentler way of teaching your children the boundaries. Abuse of children at the hands of their parents is a big problem in our culture. Be very careful on this point. Also, be very kind!

4. Does your relax-more, enjoy-more approach work with babies? Don't babies need more structure?

The answer is yes and yes! Secure babies are the ones whose parents know how to interpret the crying and meet their needs. Babies do better with regular bedtimes, regular mealtimes, that's true! And babies' needs in this area vary greatly. However, it's a mistake to live life strictly around a baby's schedule. Babies can sleep with vacuums running, in backpacks, tucked in a corner on the floor while the adults have a pizza party. Our children were always a part of what was going on. They seemed to like it that way. A loose approach to such things creates a flexible, relaxed child.

One problem many parents have is that they continue to parent in the same style they followed when their child was a baby. As the child matures, you can and should back off more.

But even babies will be happier if Mom and Dad learn to ask, "What does this child need?"

5. What about parents? Don't we have needs, too?

Parents are some of the most needy, tired, discouraged people around! Learning to meet your children's emotional, physical, and spiritual needs sounds like an overwhelming job, but it is also a gift you give yourself. It's preventive medicine. It is to family life what exercise and eating right is to the body. Build the family trust bank, learn to meet your child's needs, do the interior work of becoming attachable and trustworthy, and down the road you will have much less wear and tear in your parental role. An attached child is much less apt to be a discipline problem. Some attached parent-child pairs actually enjoy the teen years! We have found them enormously warm, affectionate, friendly, fun years in our family life. We have very few complaints. It is a myth that the teenage years have to be terrible.

And remember, I'm actually encouraging you to relax a little more, to enjoy a little more. Becoming attachable, and safe, and stable, and charming, and available, though it may be the hardest interior work you've ever tackled, is not only good for your children, but it is ultimately good for you. The parent is the great winner in the relational family.

6. How can I handle criticism from people who operate according to what "should" be happening?

Smile. Say, "That's interesting!" Give them this book to read. (Or better yet, encourage them to buy their own copy. Just kidding!) But, *do* what is in the best interest of your children. In other words, give them an ear, see if there be any wisdom in their words; if not, then ignore them graciously.

7. What if our children are raised and we were interfering parents? What can we do?

It's never too late to stop being an interfering parent. Believe me, interfering parents can drive their adult children away if any relationship remains by that point. If you sense distance in your relationship with your children, if they become upset or put off with you regularly, if they seem to tolerate being with you, it might be time to back off from the controls, unwanted opinions, and criticism, and learn to relate to and enjoy your children even in these later years of life.

I would suggest sitting down and talking about your wishes and dreams in terms of relationship with your children. Apologize if you feel it's necessary. Explain that you are still learning what it means to be a relational parent. No doubt, your children will become parents, and undoubtedly may parent your grandchildren as you parented them. They may have the very same relational problems with their kids if someone doesn't make the effort to stop the cycle of distrust and relational sickness.

I have great hope for families who care for one another. I believe that a close relationship is a desire shared by both parents and children, regardless of their ages.

It's never too late to begin to get it right!

8. What do you think about the teaching that to meet a child's needs is to give into his or her sin nature—that, for instance, a baby's crying is symptomatic of the need to be in control?

I applaud the attempt to help parents, but I find this approach biblically highly interpretive and developmentally unsound. It's a view that carries the total depravity of children to an extreme. Yes, I believe that children are born with a sin nature, but that does not mean that all their behavior is sinful. Some of the behavior that is labeled "sinful" is simply developmental.

Interestingly, this is a very old approach to raising children. John Robinson, a seventeenth-century Puritan preacher taught his congregation that "there is in all children a stubbornness, and stoutness of mind arising from natural pride, which must, in the first place, be broken and beaten down; that so the foundation of their education being laid in humility and tractableness, other virtues may in their time, be built upon."[2] The hard-line, severe approach to raising children is a throwback to a time not noted for warm family-relating. It's a prescription for interfering parenting. It's an approach that will surely drive children from their parents. We can do better. We *can* manage and nurture our children.

The idea, that to meet children's needs is to give in to their sin nature, is appealing to two types of parents. First, very insecure parents who need the assurance of a system, any system, will be attracted to such teaching. In other words, the person who thinks, "Somebody just tell me what to do!" Their basic parental insecurity will attract them to an approach that at least has some answers.

The other type of parent who will buy into this approach is the mom or dad who needs to feel in control and who only feels in control when his or her children are strictly managed. Perhaps we as parents need to be reminded that the need to control was the sin that resulted in Adam and Eve's being thrown out of the garden in the first place. It was a component of the original sin. Let me ask, in such a teaching, whose need to control is the most dominant—the child's or the parent's? Again, the cart is steaming downhill before the horse. If you want to deal with control as a sin issue—start with the parent. We need to be careful as parents that the interpretation of our children's behavior isn't coming through our own sinful need-to-control grid.

9. Why do you insist on working on parents' issues in your approach to family life?

When you start with the parent, you have adopted a preventive approach to family problems. The traditional approach has been to deal with infected, sick, family systems. There is still a need for that kind of help, but I believe the time is ripe for a healthier approach to family systems. Let's paint the picture of health. Let's heal and help the parents.

That is the place to start. Perhaps then we will have fewer children growing up to become wounded adults who also wound their own children.

10. How can you write a book about parenting before you know how your own kids turn out?

I wouldn't dare write such a book if I were guaranteeing any results in terms of how "children" would turn out. My only "guarantee" is something that only the parent has the ability to influence—that is, how the parent "turns out."

That is my focus. Anyway, it seems only logical to me that books about parenting should be about parents, not children. To answer the real underlying question, "How is this working with your kids, Valerie Bell?"—here it is: I don't blame you for being curious. Our family is close—not perfect—but well-attached. Our children have been our teachers as well as providing a home laboratory for our ideas. It's worked for us. I believe that the parents who can self-discipline themselves to become a need-meeter and trustworthy person in their children's lives will also become confident, attachable, and charming in the process. What I've been trying to emphasize is the importance of parents "turning out!"

NOTES

Chapter 1: When Something Is Missing

[1]Gilbert Kliman and Albert Rosenfeld, *Responsible Parenthood: The Child's Psyche Through the Six-Year Pregnancy* (New York: Holt, Rinehart and Winston, 1958), 201.

[2]D. W. Winnicott, *Collected Papers*, "Hate in the Countertransference," 21.

[3]Jane Lazarre, *The Mother Knot* (New York: McGraw-Hill, 1976), 59.

Chapter 2: How Do I Know If I'm a Good Parent?

[1]Naomi Feigelson Chase, *A Child Is Being Beaten* (New York: Holt, Rinehart and Winston 1975) (NA).

[2]Stephen and Janet Bly, *How to Be a Good Mom* (Chicago: Moody Press, 1988), 23.

[3]Ellen Galinsky, "The five biggest mistakes most parents make," *Ladies' Home Journal* (June 1990), 80.

Chapter 3: The Problem With Being an "In Your Face" Parent

[1]Seymour and Rhoda L. Fisher, *What We Really Know About Child Rearing: Science in Support of Effective Parenting* (New York: Basic Books, 1976), 18.

[2]Robert Karen, "Becoming Attached," *Atlantic Monthly* (February 1990), 35–70.

[3]Ibid.

Chapter 4: How To Keep Displaced Passions From Destroying Your Family Life

[1]"Dorothy Bush, president's mother: He remembered her generous love and discipline," *Chicago Tribune* (November 22, 1992) Obituary Section 4, 1.

Chapter 5: You Are the Memory

[1]Eugene H. Methvia, "Beauty and the Beast," *Reader's Digest* (February 1989), 132.

Chapter 6: Dancing With a Limp

[1]Sinichi Suzuki, *Nurtured by Love* (New York: Exposition Press 1969) 18–19.

[2]Sandra D. Wilson, *Hurt People Hurt People* (Nashville: Thomas Nelson 1993).

Chapter 7: Huckleberry Days

[1]Theodore Isaac Rubin, *Child Potential: Fulfilling Your Child's Intellectual, Emotional, and Creative Promise* (New York: Continuum 1990), 215–16.

Chapter 8: Everybody's Weird in Their Own Special Way

[1]Alice Miller, *Prisoners of Childhood: The Drama of the Gifted Child and the Search for the True Self* (New York: Basic Books 1981), 76.

[2]Cathy Lynn Grossman, "Parenting is spiraling 'out of control'," USA Today (July 28, 1993), 10.

[3]Theodore Isaac Rubin, *Child Potential: Fulfilling Your Child's Intellectual, Emotional, and Creative Promise* (New York: Continuum 1990), 252.

[4]Ibid. 194.

[5]Kliman and Rosenfeld, *Responsible Parenthood*, 213–14.

[6]Ross Campbell, *How to Really Love Your Child* (Wheaton: Scripture Press 1977), 21.

[7]Elsie Broussard and M. S. S. Hartner, "Maternal Perception of the Neonate as Related to Development." *Child Psychiatry and Human Development*, *Vol. 1*, 1970.

Chapter 9: Heat's On!

[1]Robert W. Firestone, *Compassionate Child-Rearing: An In-Depth Approach to Optimal Parenting* (New York: Plenum Press 1990), 50.

[2]Carol Kleiman, "How to Survive a Big Bad Boss," *Chicago Tribune*, Section 8, September 12, 1993.

[3]Joseph Sjostrom, "Tape of teen describes killing of parents," *Chicago Tribune*, Section 2, September 14, 1993.

[4]Tom Wolfe, "Points to Ponder," *Reader's Digest*, March 1991, 161.

Chapter 10: Not Perfect But Present

[1]Barbara Dafoe Whitehead, "Dan Quayle Was Right," *The Atlantic*, April 1993, 47–84.

[2]Ellen Goodman, "A missing father can create a void that can't be filled," *Chicago Tribune*, Tempo Section, April 25, 1992, 4.

³Ibid.

⁴Miriam Neff, *Helping Teens in Crisis* (Wheaton: Tyndale House, 1993), 52.

Chapter 11: The Healing Power of Touch

¹Ross Campbell, *How to Really Love Your Child* (Wheaton: Scripture Press, 1977), 79.

Chapter 13: When Going Back to Egypt Seems Appealing

¹Foster Cline, "Understanding and treating the severely disturbed child," Evergreen, CO: Evergreen Consultants in Human Behavior.

Appendix

¹Karen Brandon, "Ignorance about kids can unleash deadly discipline," *Chicago Tribune*, October 8, 1993, 1.

²Joy Day Buel and Richard Buel, Jr., *The Way of Duty* (New York: W. W. Norton, 1984), 8.

MOTHERS OF

MOPS®

PRESCHOOLERS

MOPS IS....

MOPS stands for Mothers of Preschoolers, a program designed for mothers with children under school age. These women come from different backgrounds and lifestyles, yet have similar needs and a shared desire to be the best mothers they can be.

A MOPS group provides a caring, accepting atmosphere for today's mothers of preschoolers. Here she has an opportunity to share concerns, explore areas of creativity, and hear instruction that equips her for the responsibilities of family and community. The MOPS program also includes MOPPETS, a program providing a loving, learning experience for children.

More than 2,000 MOPS groups meet in churches throughout the United States, Canada, and several other countries, to meet the needs of more than 70,000 women.

To find out if there is a MOPS group near you, or if you're interested in general information regarding MOPS, please write or call: MOPS International, P.O. Box 102200, Denver, CO 80250–2200. Phone: 303–733–5353 or 800–929–1287. Fax: 303–733–5770. E-mail: info@MOPS.org. Web site: http://www.mops.org.

To learn how to start a MOPS group, call 1–888–910–MOPS.